Development
and Globalisation

Daring to Think Differently

Development and Globalisation

Daring to Think Differently

Yash Tandon

Foreword by
Benjamin W. Mkapa

Pambazuka Press
An imprint of Fahamu Books

Published 2009 by Pambazuka Press, an imprint of Fahamu Books
Cape Town, Dakar, Nairobi and Oxford
www.pambazukapress.org   www.fahamubooks.org   www.pambazuka.org

and

South Centre
Geneva
www.southcentre.org

Fahamu Books, 2nd floor, 51 Cornmarket Street, Oxford OX1 3HA, UK
Fahamu Kenya, PO Box 47158, 00100 GPO, Nairobi, Kenya
Fahamu Senegal, 9 Cité Sonatel 2, POB 25021, Dakar-Fann, Dakar, Senegal
Fahamu South Africa, c/o 27A Esher St, Claremont, 7708,
Cape Town, South Africa

South Centre, CP 228, 1211 Geneva 19, Switzerland

First edition published by South Centre 2009
Second edition published by Pambazuka Press and South Centre 2009

British Library Cataloguing in Publication Data
A catalogue record for this book is available from the British Library

ISBN: 978-1-906387-51-8   second edition, paperback
ISBN: 978-1-906387-52-5   ebook

Manufactured on demand by Lightning Source

Contents

Foreword

Benjamin W. Mkapa
President of Tanzania 1995-2005

Former US Vice-President Dick Cheney is reported to have said, 'We are an Empire; when we act we create our own reality.' In response, we from the South say, 'We emerge out of imperial domination; when we think and act collectively, we create another reality.'

The 'reality' created by the empire is now a thoroughly discredited one. At the root of the present financial crisis is the system of speculative financialised capitalism and the wealth 'bubbles' being created out of it. The sweat-based wealth of the South, created from the labour and industry of billions of people working there in small farms and domestic manufacturing, is unable to compete with the speculation-based wealth being generated from Wall Street. The existing power asymmetries, for instance within the World Trade Organisation, further diminish the value of what is being currently produced from the South. The increasing control by the North of intellectual property rights threatens the future output from these countries. This is the fundamental reason behind the South's poverty and inequity in the global system. Such a state of affairs is neither just nor sustainable. The reality that the South Centre seeks to create is a world of equity, justice, fairness and peace.

The establishment of the South Centre was a milestone in the development of an independent voice of the countries of the South, most of whom had emerged from colonial and semi-colonial domination in the decades following the Second World War. Within the United Nations there are agencies set up to serve the South, such as the United Nations Conference on Trade and Development (UNCTAD), and there are several independent intergovernmental agencies of the South, such as the G24 and the G15 and the Non-Aligned Movement. However, the South Centre is the only intergovernmental organisation of the South with the capacity to go beyond research and provide hands-on expertise for negotiations on matters of concern to the South boosted by its status as an observer to many intergovernmental forums, including the United Nations General Assembly. Above all, it is the Southern intergovernmental independent think tank that seeks to provide an alternative perspective on matters ranging from development, trade and intellectual property to climate change and global governance. This is its strength.

In the pages that follow the executive director of the South Centre from 2005 to 2009 has put his ideas on an alternative paradigm of development as a counter to the dominant imperial paradigm of the North. These are essays written as editorials for the South Centre's fortnightly *South Bulletin: Reflections and Foresights.* The editorials were written as events unfolded, and not with the benefit of hindsight. Many of them are very critical of the present system of global economic and political governance, but they are not critical for the sake of it. They offer an alternative paradigm, an alternative perspective, often with concrete suggestions on how to move these issues forward. Well before some of the world's leaders began to talk about the need for a second Bretton Woods conference, for example, the *Bulletin* was proposing it.

Some of the ideas may well be before their time, such as that of returning to the open solar energy system in order to reverse the over three hundred years of a fossil-fuel based closed system that is primarily the cause of global warming, but it is difficult to reject summarily the logic behind the idea. Some of the ideas are practical and doable, but there are serious psychological and institutional obstacles to implementing them, such as the idea of ending dependence on aid and working against the existing power asymmetries. Again, it is difficult to dismiss the logic behind the ideas.

As language goes, so does thought. It is one of the running threads of the editorials to question the concepts which embody contemporary thought and practice and to offer alternative concepts. The received concepts of the past create models, the architecture of the dominant cognitive paradigm, and a pedagogy that determine the interpretation of facts and the analysis of 'reality' trapped in these concepts. These, then, form the basis of 'policy' analysis, that much vaulted 'science' of development which 'development experts' from the North bring to the South in the baggage called 'development aid'. What the author of these essays does is challenge these policy prescriptions and the paradigms on which they are based. We must, he says, liberate our minds from the traps of language and concepts which form the nuts and bolts of value-laden and self-serving models of the global North that now are in the throes of the crisis that it has itself created and which has now engulfed the rest of us.

These essays promise to stand the test of time. It is a promise that the South Centre must strive to uphold and fortify.

To the memory of the late Mwalimu Julius Nyerere and to all those who are engaged in promoting South-South solidarity, and North-South dialogue and understanding

Acknowledgements

A reflective book such as this, based on experiences at the South Centre, cannot be written without collective energy. To all my colleagues at the South Centre I owe deep gratitude, especially those who helped me think through these ideas and correct, refine and nuance the arguments and language of these editorials. Among these are: Aileen Kwa, Bernarditas Muller, Darlan F. Marti, Irfan Ul Haque, Khalil Hamdani, Luisa Bernal, Luisa Rodriguez, Vicente P. Yu, Xuan Li and Vikas Nath. My special thanks to Celina Iñones, Louma Atallah and Marie Merigeau for translating the editorials into French and Spanish and for making creative and valuable editorial changes. I wish to thank also Angela Muraguri, Caroline Ngome Eneme, Joseph Nanayakkara, Kwame Quansah, Li Ling Low, Nakshatra Pachauri, Vasanthan Pushparaja, Wase Musonge and Xin Cui for managing the administration and finances of the South Centre, while I was engaged on broader issues.

I am grateful to Benjamin W. Mkapa and Norman Girvan, chairman and vice-chairman respectively of the board of the South Centre, and the members of the board, for their guidance and inspiration. To my successor as executive director of the South Centre, Martin Khor, I say thank you for many evenings spent together talking and reflecting on the issues challenging the South and the South Centre.

I wish to express my deep gratitude to Vikas Nath for conceiving the idea to reproduce the editorials as a book, and for seeing it through; Xuan Zhang for her laborious work in putting the book together; and to my wife, Mary Tandon, for holding my hands and supporting and counselling me.

Unmentioned but gratefully acknowledged are the first generation of political and intellectual leaders of the countries of the South, who fought for the liberation of the South from colonial and imperial rule and whose thoughts remain a permanent legacy for future generations. Above all, my gratitude to Mwalimu Julius Kambarage Nyerere: for the inspiration and vision that gave birth to the South Centre.

Yash Tandon
Geneva, February 2009

Abbreviations

AAA	Accra Action Agenda
ACP	African, Caribbean and Pacific Countries
AIG	American International Group
AU	African Union
BCI	Basic Capabilities Index
BdS	Banco del Sur
BNDES	Banco Nacional de Desenvolvimento Econômico e Social
BRIC	Brazil, Russia, India and China
BWIs	Bretton Woods institutions
CAF	Corporate Andina de Fomento
CDOs	collateral debt obligations
CIPIH	Commission on Intellectual Property Rights, Public Health and Innovation
COP	Conference of the Parties
CSOs	Civil Society Organisations
DAC	Development Assistance Committee
DCF	Development Cooperation Forum
EC	European Commission
ECOSOC	Economic and Social Council of the United Nations
EDF	European Development Fund
EPA	Economic Partnership Agreement
ERR	exchange rate regime
EU	European Union
FAO	Food and Agriculture Organisation of the United Nations
FDI	Foreign Direct Investment
FfD	Financing for Development
FIAN	FoodFirst Information and Action Network
FTA	free trade agreement/free trade area
GATT	General Agreement on Tariffs and Trade
GD	Great Depression
GGDP	Global Governance for Development Programme
GHG	greenhouse gas
GMO	genetically modified organism
GPG	global public good

IAASTD	International Assessment of Agricultural Knowledge, Science and Technology for Development
IAKP	Innovation and Access to Knowledge Programme
IDB	Inter-American Development Bank
IFAD	International Fund for Agricultural Development
IGO	intergovernmental organisation
IMF	International Monetary Fund
IP	intellectual property
IPCC	Intergovernmental Panel on Climate Change
JCC	Joint Coordinating Committee
LDCs	least developed countries
LTCM	Long Term Capital Management
MDB	multilateral development banks
MDGs	Millennium Development Goals
NAFTA	North American Free Trade Agreement
NAM	Non-Aligned Movement
NAMA	Non-Agricultural Market Access
NCR	northern corporate rightholder
NINA	No Income, No Assets
ODA	official development assistance
OECD	Organisation of Economic Cooperation and Development
OPEC	Organisation of Oil Exporting Countries
OREC	Organisation of Rice Exporting Countries
PDAE	Paris Declaration on Aid Effectiveness
PRSP	Poverty Reduction Strategy Paper
RMA	regional monetary agreement
SAFE	WCO Framework of Standards to Secure and Facilitate Global Trade
SAP	Structural Adjustment Programme
SECURE	Provisional Standards Employed by Customs for Uniform Rights Enforcement
SPV	special purpose vehicle
TDP	Trade for Development Programme
TINA	There is No Alternative
TNC	transnational corporation
TRIP	Trade Related Intellectual Property Right
UN	United Nations

UNCTAD	United Nations Conference on Trade and Development
UNECA	United Nations Economic Commission for Africa
UNFCCC	United Nations Framework Convention on Climate Change
UNICEF	United Nations Children's Fund
UNIDO	United Nations Industry and Development Organisation
WAIPA	World Association of Investment Promotion Agencies
WCO	World Customs Organisation
WFP	World Food Programme
WHO	World Health Organisation
WIF	World Investment Forum
WIPO	World Intellectual Property Organisation
WPAE	Working Party on Aid Effectiveness
WTO	World Trade Organisation

Part I
Imperatives of paradigm shift

1

Rethinking the development paradigm

Introduction

The German philosopher Karl Mannheim defined ideology as the total system of thought held by society's ruling groups that obscure the real conditions and thereby preserve the status quo. He said that in class-divided societies a special stratum of individuals 'whose only capital consisted in their education' develop their ideas to advance the interests of different classes. Among them are those that serve the ruling classes; they provide the knowledge that forms the kernel of the ruling ideology, the dominant *Weltanschauung*. These are opposed by another stratum that challenges the ruling orthodoxy, including the production of knowledge. Mannheim argued that the prevailing ideology makes the ruling groups opposed to knowledge that would threaten their continued domination.

To his credit Alan Greenspan, the former head of the Federal Reserve of the United States, admitted that he found a 'flaw in the free market theory'. When asked, 'You mean that your view of the world, your ideology, was not right, it was not working?' Greenspan replied, 'Absolutely, precisely. You know that's precisely the reason I was shocked, because I have been going for 40 years or more with the very considerable evidence that it was working exceptionally well.' This should be a lesson to the leaders of the countries of the South when they rush to the International Monetary Fund (IMF) and the World Bank, or when they go, cap in hand, to get 'aid' (known by the official misnomer as 'development assistance cooperation'). Packaged in 'aid' is the anti-development paradigm of these institutions. These are institutions of ideological obscurantism; they are part of the problem and not part of the solution.

The American physicist, Thomas Kuhn, in his classic *The Structure of Scientific Revolutions*, argued that science evolves through alternating 'normal' and 'revolutionary' phases. Kuhn described normal science as 'puzzle-solving'. Because its puzzles and their solutions are 'familiar science', the theorists seek to solve the puzzles within the existing paradigm. Revolutionary science, on the other hand, seeks to provide new thinking outside the existing paradigm (a paradigm shift), thinking outside the box. Of course, Kuhn's book received a hostile reception during his time because as Mannheim explained to us, the ruling intellectual oligarchy fights hard to protect their orthodoxies. The challenge that the modern intelligentsia faces, then, is to try and produce knowledge that will liberate the people as well as their political leaders from the prevailing obscurantist mindset.

The essays in this chapter were written at various times as editorials for the South Centre fortnightly bulletin, *Reflections and Foresights*. They seek to analyse the backward and anti-developmental character of present institutions and mainstream 'development' policies, and advocate the need for alternative knowledge systems. The first essay, 'Neoliberal obscurantism and its ill-fated children', challenges those leaders in the South who think that their 'sovereign funds' or reserves can be used to save the financially stressed IMF. It argues that bailing out the IMF would be '...the greatest irony of our present times – a parody of History. It would be like allowing the fox back into the henhouse'.

The second essay, 'The global financial meltdown and lessons for the South', agrees with the now well-recognised fact that the market does not have a self-correcting mechanism. Those who argue that the South must be forced to liberalise, and if people suffer that is just 'regrettable collateral damage', have the same flawed reasoning that Israel has used in its war against the people of Gaza. Western leaders do not pretend anymore that they comprehend the nature of the present financial crisis. They talk of removing 'toxic' or cancerous paper from the system. The whole system, we argue, is metastasised, has become cancerous. It is thus not simply a question of 'market failure': Western leaders are facing a crisis of cognitive paradigmatic failure. They simply do not know what has hit them and how to get out of the mess.

Therefore, those global institutions that pretend to be the 'knowledge' banks of the world such as the World Bank and the International Monetary Fund (IMF) must self-destruct, or be radically reformed (which, given the present geopolitical configuration, is unlikely). The South Centre, to our knowledge, was the first intergovernmental body to argue for a new Bretton Woods conference. 'Time for a new Bretton Woods conference', written on 16 October 2008, reflects on how times have changed:

- The US-dominated, unicentric world is now replaced by a polycentric world.
- The neoliberal ideology and the so-called 'Washington Consensus' are in tatters; the ships that were supposed to lift are sinking, and the US 'Titanic' is wobbling.
- The Doha round, in which the North had put so much faith, is frozen; the South has successfully put the development horse before the trade cart.
- The IMF and the World Bank are desperately searching for survival strategies; last year's IMF's voting reform was a travesty that both recognised IMF's own legitimacy deficit, and its failure to do anything about it.
- The West is trying desperately to monopolise corporate knowledge in the form of intellectual property, but is facing serious resistance from the South in the World Intellectual Property Organisation (WIPO) and other similar institutions.
- Climate change is a hot issue for the North, and the World Bank is trying to undermine the United Nations Framework Convention on Climate Change (UNFCCC), but for the South it is a development issue for survival and poverty eradication.
- The financial meltdown is worse than that of the 1930s. The Smoot-Hatley Tariff Act triggered the Great Depression (GD1), but the collapsing 'real' economies (and not just the banks) and rising unemployment in the West, and the re-emergence of protectionism (stigmatised as worse than crime when the South sought to protect their economies) portend worse things to come with GD2.

However, we are not optimistic that things will change any time soon: Why? Because the imperial powers have buried their heads in the sand and do not wish to recognise the historical necessity for a fresh start. After every major war, there is reconstruction. This happened at the end of the First and Second World Wars. A third war, partly avoided on account of the nuclear threat, has taken the form of the North's 'war' on the South in the name of globalisation. This war has not yet ended. The initiative this time has to come from people, bottom–up.

In 'Ecuador's proposal on the financial crisis' we argue that the President Bush-initiated G20 meeting in Washington DC following the financial collapse produced a declaration that boils down to blaming market failure, insufficient coordination of macroeconomic policies and inadequate structural reforms. It lacks empirical correspondence to the reality and theoretical depth. In contrast to the globalised integration model advocated by the G20, Pedro Paez Pérez, Ecuador's minister of economic policy coordination advocated a regional model, including 'decoupling from the dollar's crisis logic' at the Interactive Panel of the United Nations General Assembly. Pérez's perspective is similar to my own in my recently published book *Ending Aid Dependency* (see www.aidexit.org).

'Decoupling' is the idea that the economies of the industrialised and the developing countries are no longer closely related and that a slowdown in the former can be offset by growth in the latter, especially in the BRIC countries – Brazil, Russia, India and China. This is only half-true. The BRIC countries partially escaped from the sub-prime housing crisis because their banking systems were not that deeply integrated with the global banking system. Their economies are now suffering to the extent that these are integrated in the global trading and investment networks. However, we argue that if decoupling has not occurred, it is *imperative* for the South that it does. In one of the earliest editorials (in October 2007) we engaged in the debate that had just started in the media on decoupling. In 'The decoupling imperative', we argued, following the sub-prime crisis but well before it escalated into present financial crisis, that '…the sub-prime crisis shows that it is imperative for the South, above all, to decouple or "selectively disengage" from the contagious effects of Western financial and speculative markets. These and asset pricing mechanisms are even more risky for the South than terms of trade. Decoupling, if it has not happened, is now an economic and political imperative for the South'.

The leaders of the South who thought there was no option but to integrate in a globalised world, and even those who talked about 'fair globalisation', must step back and review their positions.

In this context, in the 'Banco del Sur – another step towards decoupling' editorial we welcomed the launch of the Bank of the South in December 2007 and challenged Western criticism that it would not take off because it would be 'dominated by Chavez'. On the contrary, we argued that the Banco del Sur has the potential to grow into a continental bank for Latin America. If followed through, its logical and historical necessity would free the region from the IMF, the World Bank and the Inter-American Development Bank conditionalities that have for decades chained their economies to the failed macroeconomic policies of the Bretton Woods institutions.

In 'A new geopolitical double paradox stalks the world' we examine the development of an interesting paradox in the global political economy. While a large number of countries in the South are getting deeper into the mire of poverty and marginalisation, there are some countries in the South that are now engaged in recapitalising Northern economies which are in the throes of a deepening credit squeeze. The implications of this paradox have not been fully understood let alone analysed. Plenoxia – the desire to have more and more, in this case of wealth – has seized the psychology of the newly rich in the rich countries of the South as well as the rich in the older countries of the North. Is its one consequence the forced anorexia of the poorer nations and, worse, the poorest people within the poor nations? Is there something missing here? Should not the relationship between countries of the South (South–South relations) be built on a different model from the greed and profit-driven model of the North–South relations?

We partly address this question in the piece on 'The Non-Aligned Movement and the collapse of the Doha round', written in July 2008, when we witnessed the collapse of the Doha round of trade negotiations at the same time as the 118 member states of the Non-Aligned Movement concluded a successful ministerial meeting in Teheran. These are symptomatic events. The first is the futile attempt by the power holders of the old order to sustain that order, including an outdated and unfair trading regime. The second is the countervailing power emerging in the South that is challenging the old order and trying to mould a South–South relationship built on the Bandung principles of solidarity and non-interference in the internal affairs of sovereign countries. We live in a twilight zone – the world is going through a period of transition, from one order to another.

These are the major themes of this chapter. Although some were written before the present financial crisis boiled over, the editorials have sought to expose the essential character of the present imperialist-dominated global economic system – fragile, ineffective and illegitimate. The basic thrust of the arguments in the editorials has been to caution Southern leaders and peoples against the dangers hidden behind the ideology of neoliberal globalisation. This ideology has for too long limited the mindset of our political leaders to 'puzzle-solving' (as Kuhn put it) within the existing failed paradigm. Another paradigm of development, it is argued in these editorials, has become a historical necessity.

Neoliberal obscurantism and its ill-fated children

1 November 2008

On close questioning from the US Congressional hearings Mr Alan Greenspan, who for 18 years has been at the apex of the Federal Reserve of the United States, admitted that he found a 'flaw in the free market theory'. Representative Waxman relentlessly pursued this in his questions. You, mean, he asked, 'that your view of the world, your ideology, was not right, it was not working?' Greenspan replied, 'Absolutely, precisely. You know that's precisely the reason I was shocked, because I have been going for 40 years or more with the very considerable evidence that it was working exceptionally well.'[1]

Mr Greenspan should be commended for his honesty. This is more than one can say for literally hundreds of ideologists, clustered around some of the best universities in the North and also in the South, and economists in the World Bank and the International Monetary Fund (IMF). From their cloistered and hallowed sanctuaries they design policies for the distressed nations of the South whose leaders rush to them for advice and financial bailouts. They should be warned that in their rush to the IMF and the World Bank they are not necessarily helping their people. These are institutions of ideological obscurantism; they are part of the problem and not part of the solution.

The German philosopher Karl Mannheim defined ideology as the total system of thought held by society's ruling groups that obscure the real conditions and thereby preserve the status quo. In his classic *Ideology and Utopia: An Introduction to the Sociology of Knowledge*, he analysed the relationship between sociology and social policy and the role of the intelligentsia. Borrowing from Karl Marx, Mannheim argued that the ideological structure of thought is conditioned by the class structure of society. He went on to say that in class-divided societies a special stratum of individuals 'whose only capital consisted in their education' develop their ideas to advance the interests of different classes. Among them are those that serve the ruling classes; they provide the knowledge that forms the kernel of the ruling ideology, the dominant *Weltanschauung*. These are opposed by another stratum that challenges the ruling orthodoxy, including the production of knowledge. Mannheim argued that the prevailing ideology makes the ruling groups opposed to knowledge that would threaten their continued domination.

We are at this critical moment in history. We are at a crossroads between the neoclassical theory that has ruled for nearly 40 years (as Greenspan says) and produced the failed ideology of neoliberalism on the one hand, and on the other hand the challenge that the modern intelligentsia faces to produce knowledge that would liberate the people as well as their political leaders from the prevailing obscurantist mindset.

So where do we start? We start with Mr Alan Greenspan's honest admission about the flawed ideology of the free market. The commonplace understanding of the market is a place where people come to buy or sell. The capitalist market, however, is much more complex and works at many different levels. What we need to understand, to start with, is that in the present phase of the evolution of capitalism, finance is the king. Everything that enters the market is financialised. Consider the housing market in the United States, for example. What explains the housing bubble that burst in September 2007, leading to what is known as the sub-prime crisis?

Simply explained, it starts with the financing of house purchase. House buyers were persuaded by the banks to borrow from them at cheap rates and with long redemption dates. The banks had too much liquidity on their hands – not hard cash, but fictitious money (for every dollar in cash, banks can 'create' many more dollars as credit). They targeted the housing market. Until five or ten years ago, the banks would take the houses as collateral against which to make the loans. But capitalism thrives on greed; it is its basic nature – like it is for the leopard to kill. So the banks went for the kill. They developed innovative ways of doubling or quadrupling their profits by collateralising the mortgages. How did they do it?

Ordinarily, investment banks deal in stocks and bonds. These, depending on their performance, are rated by the rating agencies (such as Moodys) as AAA (triple A) for the best performers and CCC for weak performers. Driven by the profit motive (greed), and using new sophisticated computer models, the investment banks packaged housing mortgages with triple A stock and created new commercial instruments called collateral debt obligations (CDOs). These included bonds classed as senior debt, mezzanine debt, subordinate debt and equity, and some unrated securities, or junk bonds, which the present US Secretary of the Treasury Henry Paulson, from hindsight, described as 'toxic' paper. These CDOs were then sold as collateralised bonds in the global market. By the year 2007, the US banks had issued approximately $2 trillion worth of CDOs. According to the IMF, in the US financial sector $23 trillion is subject to potential writedowns. The estimated losses are $1.4 trillion and of these, losses on sub-prime loans are estimated at only $50 billion while estimated losses on CDOs/securities are $980 billion. It would seem there was very little 'prime' or even 'sub-prime' in the CDOs.

Furthermore, worse was to come: the banks also removed some of their assets from their balance sheets and transferred these to the CDOs portfolio. Why did they do this? They did this to escape from the regulatory capital requirements such as those imposed by their own national regulatory authorities and the Basle Convention. Some of them used what they called special purpose vehicles (SPVs). These are special companies ostensibly aimed at protecting specific assets, but in reality they became a way of hiding debts, as we saw with the collapse of Enron.

Today, with hindsight, the US and European governments are getting back to regulating the banks and even nationalising some of them, raising the spectre of 'socialism' in the public media. Remove the technicalities and statistics from the above paragraphs, and the reality stares one in the face that the CDOs were really synthetic bonds, like synthetic coffee. They contained some triple A corporate bonds mixed with a lot of junk, backed by nothing substantial other than synthetic money. The banks were heading for the rocks. Had Alan Greenspan consulted better economists he would not have had such a 'shock'. He would have been told that no amount of obfuscation and obscurantism by neoliberal theorists could hide the reality that under the present phase of financialised capitalism – capitalism not run by the priority of production over finance, but of finance over production – the global economy is heading for the rocks.

The story does not stop with the housing bubble. Greed drove investment banks from houses to oil, metals, cereals and other commodities. Neoclassical theory says that prices are determined in the market by 'supply and demand'. This may be so in the long run, but in the short run, the prices of commodities, including food, are set by the futures market in places like the Chicago Mercantile Exchange where they trade in futures and forward contracts based on pure speculation. Food that is not even seeded in the ground, let alone harvested, is financialised through the creation of tradeable bonds in the futures market. Much of what has happened to the housing market in the US has happened to the food prices in the global market. Some neoliberal theorists now put the blame on the rising demand for food from countries like China and India. They are obscuring the reality. They are not looking where they should be.

What, then, is the moral of the story? What can the political and intellectual leaders in the South do about the obscurantism of neoliberal theorists and their ill-begotten children?

Let us learn from another philosopher, this time the American physicist Thomas Kuhn. In his classic *The Structure of Scientific Revolutions*, Kuhn argued that science evolves through alternating 'normal' and 'revolutionary' phases. The revolutionary phases differ qualitatively from normal science. Kuhn described normal science as 'puzzle-solving'. Because its puzzles and their solutions are 'familiar science', the theorists seek to solve the puzzles within the existing paradigm. Revolutionary science, on the other hand, seeks to provide new thinking outside the existing paradigm (a paradigm shift), thinking outside the box. Of course, Kuhn's book received much hostile reception during his time because as Mannheim explained to us, the ruling intellectual oligarchy fight hard to protect their orthodoxies.

So where do we begin? We begin by thinking outside the neoliberal paradigm, not only in relation to theory, but in terms of today's practical problems. Intellectuals should ask themselves whether the 'puzzles' created by the financialisation of capitalism can be solved within the existing paradigm. As for the political leadership in the South, they should use their reserve or sovereign funds (if they have them, such as China, India and the Gulf states) to create regional banking and credit systems that would protect countries in the region from external and foreign exchange shocks and to develop regional currencies. The recent decision by ASEAN+3 to create an $80 billion regional pooling mechanism to safeguard regional financial stability is a step in the right direction.

The danger some of the larger countries of the South face in the efforts by the North to revive the IMF is that by being co-opted they could become part of the problem and not part of the solution. They might be persuaded to help bail out the IMF so that the latter would then bail out others in the South. If they do, then this would be the greatest irony of our present times – a parody of history. It would be like allowing the fox back into the henhouse.

Note

1 *International Herald Tribune*, 24 October 2008.

The global financial meltdown and lessons for the South

1 October 2008

The debt-financed US-led global economy is crumbling. What lessons can the leaders of the South learn from the present meltdown of the Western capitalist system?

The first lesson, surely, is that contrary to mainstream thinking, the market does not have a self-corrective mechanism. In the present crisis the 'market makers' are watching nervously from the sidelines as the US Congress and the politicians huddle together to see how to bail out the banks. The leaders of the South have been instructed in innumerable reports and policy recommendations by 'experts' from the International Monetary Fund (IMF), the World Bank, and the World Trade Organisation (WTO) as well as Northern politicians that they should let their economies be ruled by the market. As recently as 9 February 2008 EU Trade Commissioner Peter Mandelson spoke at Cambridge arguing, essentially, that if the South does not liberalise its markets, it must be forced to do so through applying the WTO rules of reciprocity. This is part of the neoliberal rhetoric. If businesses fail, let them. All state intervention or cushioning is like nursing dying patients. In the course of time, the countries will find their comparative 'niche' advantage in the global chain of production and trade. In the meantime, if people suffer they must be made to understand that this is the necessary pain of adjustment. If millions of smallholder food- and cotton-producing farmers in the South perish because free trade demands further liberalisation of the global market, then it is just bad luck for them and their families. Paradoxically, this logic has now been stood on its head when it comes to bailing out the monolithic financial institutions in the North and protecting the jobs and home mortgages of those who, through no fault of their own, have become victims of the sub-prime mortgage crisis.

The second lesson of the present financial crisis is that people matter. It is election time in the US, and the people who have been ignored for so long suddenly matter. However, there is a difference between the North and the South. In the North the people wait for elections, in the South they go instantly to the streets. In the North people are on the sidelines, passively waiting for the politicians and bankers to decide their fate. In the South people take matters in their own hands and bring abrupt changes in government (including military coups), or they vote with their feet and migrate to neighbouring countries or to the North. These are generalisations, but generalisations contain a germ of truth. People in the North and South have different circumstances and they act as their circumstances and institutions allow. For the North to argue that the South must copy Northern systems of governance and democracy is to ignore the reality of history.

A third lesson is that crisis is endemic to the capitalist system. In explaining the present financial crisis, Walden Bello, senior analyst of Focus on the Global South, has argued that its roots lie in the overproduction of capital and underconsumption by the masses. This is indeed so. On the one hand, capital is overcapital-ising through the creation of mountains of fictitious capital such as, for example, collaterised debt obligations (CDOs are clever instruments that mix triple-A-rated securities with junk bonds – or 'toxic paper' – and packaged as collateralised securities; these are at the heart of the sub-prime crisis). On the other hand, even as the corporate elite earn millions of dollars (Goldman Sach's 30,000 employees each earned an average of $600,000 per year, and its CEO $68 million), millions of people throughout the United States are in deep personal debt and cannot put two meals together or meet their health bills or mortgage commitments.

Besides overproduction of capital and underconsumption by masses, the fundamental cause of the financial crisis is that capi-talism, in essence, is an anarchical system. Adam Smith's invisible hand, in which everybody's greed is the basis for social good, is a veritable formula for anarchy. Schumpeter idealised capital-ism as a process of 'constructive destruction'. History, however, has seen appalling destruction of people's lives, cultures and the environment (whose end we have not yet seen) caused by neolib-eral policies. It is a questionable compliment to Adam Smith that his theories have lasted so long in various forms and guises, the latest being its neoliberal phase. But time has come now, finally, to put the ghost of Adam Smith to rest. From sub-prime rate cri-sis to direct state intervention and nationalisation of banks and their global assets, there is now no turning back to neoliberalism. Neoliberalism, too, is dead or dying a slow death.

A fourth lesson to learn is to recognise that the leaders of the North and of finance capital do not pretend any more that they fully comprehend the nature of this crisis. They admit that they do not know what the 'true value' is behind the inflated and debt-ridden commercial paper (like CDOs). They talk of removing toxic or cancerous paper from the system, but nobody knows how. Nobody knows how to save the body from the cancerous cells. The whole body is metastasised. There is, in other words, a crisis of cognitive paradigmatic failure. They simply do not know. It is a collapse of the paradigm that informed their understanding of themselves. They might put Humpty-Dumpty back together again (although nobody knows how), but the cancerous growth will surely continue. The system is heading towards a cataclysmic demise.

And here is the fifth lesson for the leaders of the South. For too long they have also accepted neoliberalism as the cure-all for the ills of poverty and deprivation in their countries. Some have found vindication in wealth creation that has put them in league with *Fortune* magazine's world's richest 100. But the people in their countries are suffering, and are now resisting. In the people's rejection of Tata's attempt to locate the new car industry in Bengal in India lies a symbolic expression of where the future is heading – and the leaders of the South had best heed this signal.

The leaders of the South who thought there was no option but to integrate in a globalised world, and even those who talked about 'fair globalisation', must step back and review their positions. In issue 3 of the *South Bulletin*, published on 1 November 2007, we argued editorially that '…the sub-prime crisis shows that it is imperative for the South, above all, to decouple or "selectively disengage" from the contagious effects of Western financial and speculative markets. These and asset pricing mechanisms are even more risky for the South than terms of trade. Decoupling, if it has not happened, is now an economic and political imperative for the South.'

The captains of industry and the holders of sovereign wealth funds in the South might be tempted to pick up assets and banks in the North on the cheap, although it is unlikely that having nationalised these, the governments of the North will allow these to be 'denationalised' to the extent that their ownership and control pass over to the financial and industrial giants and national governments of the South. China may be the world's workshop, India its communications centre, and Brazil its farm, but to allow China, India and Brazil to control the commanding heights of the economy of the North would, for the North, be suicidal. Southern capital could instead be better, and more profitably, used by investing in the development of the South and so improve the South's collective ability to shape its own destiny.

Over the next decades what we shall be witnessing between especially the older industrialised countries of the North and the newly industrialising countries of the South is an intensified competition for global resources – oil, fuel, land, forests, water, minerals and so on. Capitalism has been a predatory system of over 400 years' duration, with dire ecological consequences: global warming, drought, water scarcity, soil degradation, the death of forests, the melting of the glaciers, the destabilisation of the Asian monsoon, etc. These have already caused eco-induced migration (so we now have environmental refugees as well as economic and political ones) and land-use conflicts. What we are witnessing is not just the melting of the global financial market. What we are witnessing is the meltdown of the capitalist and ecological systems. So the final lesson to learn from the present conjunctural crisis of the financial system is that the leaders of the South must now take the lead, in discussion with their peoples, to try and build a different world based on a different paradigm in contrast to the 400-year-old capitalist paradigm that is now meeting its denouement in the North.

Time for a new Bretton Woods conference

16 October 2008

The long drawn out process leading to the Financing for Development (FfD) review conference to be held in Doha at the end of November is reaching its final stage. A draft outcome document is already out although negotiations on it are more or less frozen until Doha. It would be unrealistic to factor effects of the Western financial meltdown into the draft text. Never very enthusiastic about the FfD addressing systemic issues, the US, the European Union and Japan are likely to play down the crisis.

That is one limiting factor about the Doha FfD review. The other is that the outcomes of multilateral negotiations do not necessarily reflect the reality on the ground; they reflect, rather, a certain diplomatic reality. Diplomatic realities are 'negotiated truths' between states in the global system of asymmetrically positioned power relationships. These 'truths' may have only a partial correspondence with existential truths about reality on the ground. In the negotiated, diplomatic truth of the outcome text, the FfD conference will try to craft a language that addresses the concerns of the South without embarrassing the North. It might repeat the ritual of promoting the good of globalisation while minimising its negatives. It might also repeat the mantra about how official development assistance (ODA) has been good for the South and how efforts must be made by the developed countries to meet their 0.7 per cent obligation, and refer to the Accra Action Agenda (AAA) that endorsed the Paris Declaration on Aid Effectiveness (PDAE) as a 'step forward'.

The financial meltdown of the developed North has affected the South too, but the South's partial decoupling from the North has somewhat lessened the impact. But at Doha nobody is likely to mention this, because the ruling ideology still favours 'globalisation' rather than decoupling. The collapsing financial infrastructure of the North and their banks' undignified rush for their governments' support is hardly an encouraging moment for seeking finances from the North for development in the South. Ironically, the North is already seeking funds from the South (including sovereign wealth funds) to recapitalise their banks. The final document might refer to the systemic risks of the unregulated global financial market and invite the Bretton Woods institutions (BWIs) and the Basel Committee on Banking Supervision to strengthen their capacity to regulate this market. But it is unlikely that FfD will come up with any fundamental rethinking about the BWIs or about the global financial infrastructure.

Nonetheless, whatever the final outcome at Doha, it is becoming evidently clear that the time has come for a new Bretton Woods-kind of conference (this time probably somewhere in the South – Beijing?). The reality on the ground has changed. However, before we consider this, let us recall the reality that shaped the discourse that led to the FfD strategy at Monterrey and what it really achieved.

One aspect of that reality was the end of the cold war and the near monopoly of power in the hands of the only superpower left. The second was 9/11, which made America pathologically insecure and laid the basis for its 'war on terror'. The shadow of 9/11 formed the backdrop for the launch of the Doha round of trade negotiations in November 2001. Trade liberalisation had become part of the anti-terrorist arsenal. The US had reasoned that those who were opposed to Doha would give solace to the terrorists. A World Bank study at the time had suggested that further global trade liberalisation would lift an extra 300 million people out of poverty by 2015. The Doha round was the expression of an ultimate faith in the neoliberal ideology of the institutions of global governance that include the World Bank, the International Monetary Fund (IMF), the World Trade Organisation (WTO) and the Organisation of Economic Cooperation and Development (OECD), the club of the rich 'donor' countries of the North.

Then came the FfD conference in Monterrey, Mexico, in March 2002. So desperate was the need to defend neoliberal ideology at Monterrey that its collapse in Argentina only a month earlier was calculatedly ignored. Argentina had faithfully followed the Washington Consensus and the dictates of the IMF and the World Bank for over two decades, but their model of development was simply routed. The economy disintegrated, bringing in its wake political and social crises. Argentina faced $155 billion debt, the highest in history until then (huge at the time, but small compared to the debt the US economy faces today). But at Monterrey the FfD negotiations went on as if Argentina's crisis did not exist, and as if the disgraceful demise of the Washington Consensus had not happened. The negotiators from both the South as well as the North decided to close their eyes to Argentina.

That was the 'diplomatic truth' of Monterrey. The underlying rationale of the Monterrey consensus on FfD was the integration of the South (especially the poor South) into the North-dominated globalised economy, and finance for development was in reality finance for globalisation. If development is the objective and finance the means, then Monterrey put the cart before the horse. In the political and diplomatic reality of Monterrey, there was, in fact, no discussion on what constituted development. Development was assumed to be based on the Washington Consensus and the Doha 'Development' round. The Monterrey 'consensus' was, in fact, on the financialisation of development instead of on the developmentalisation of finance, which is what was needed. Financialisation is now in tatters, and so the question is: How do we move from the failed experiment of Bretton Woods and of Monterrey to the future?

First, it is important to acknowledge that times have changed since 2002. Only those whose heads are buried in the sand will fail to recognise the historical necessity for a fresh start. After every major war, there is reconstruction. This happened at the end of the First and Second World Wars. A third war, partly avoided on account of the nuclear threat, has taken the form of the North's 'war' on the South in the name of globalisation. But the changed geopolitical reality can no longer be ignored. Here are some of its aspects.

One, the US-dominated unicentric world is now replaced by a polycentric world. The United States' virtual defeat in Afghanistan and Iraq – wars that have lasted longer than the Second World War – has shaken American belief in its infallibility and diminished the South's awe for the US or for its 'coalition of the willing'. The US no longer enjoys the strategic or tactical high ground that it still had at Doha in 2001 and at Monterrey in 2002.

Two, the neoliberal ideology and the Washington Consensus are in tatters. Globalisation, once touted as an inevitable phenomenon, like gravity in physics, is exposed for what it always was – a project of the North to globalise its corporate power. The ships that were supposed to lift with the rising tide of globalisation are sinking; and indeed, the 'Titanic US' is wobbling in the sea of global definancialisation.

Three, the Doha round in which the North had put so much faith is in the freezer. The South, pushed by pressure from people below, has successfully hitched its wagon to 'development' and brought the trade negotiations back to Doha's developmental promise. The South has moved the horse to the front of the cart. It is a reversal of both Doha and Monterrey. Financing is now, or should be, the servant of development and not its master.

Four, the IMF and the World Bank are desperately searching for survival strategies. They have become largely irrelevant. The efforts by the OECD to bring the PDAE to the fore is a belated attempt to throw the World Bank a lifeline. PDAE's endorsement in Accra in September 2008 is a temporary phenomenon. It is a matter of time before its underlying agenda – that of continuing collective neocolonial control by the North over the aid recipient countries of the South – will be exposed. The IMF's belated effort to reform its voting formula in recognition of the new geopolitical reality, and recent proposals in the World Bank for reforms, are a travesty of the reform that is actually needed.

Five, climate change has become the biggest issue, at least for the North. For the South, it is simply another facet of their continuing development and poverty eradication challenge. One of the most contentious issues on climate change is how to finance the huge costs involved in moving to a new, low-carbon global economy. Once again, aided and abetted by the North, the World Bank is seeking a role by positioning itself as the conduit for Northern funds for climate financing. But in so doing, it and the North are ignoring the United Nations Framework Convention on Climate Change (UNFCCC), under which the provision of new, additional, adequate and predictable finance from the North is a legally binding commitment to be channelled through the UNFCCC's financial mechanism.

Finally, of course, there is the meltdown of the global financial infrastructure. It is no ordinary crisis. It is compared to the 1929 Wall Street crisis, but it could be much worse. In 1930 the US Congress passed the Smoot–Hatley Tariff Act, triggering the Great Depression by creating trade barriers. Today, the Paulson bailout for favoured banks and corporations such as the American International Group (AIG), which followed the Darwinian collapse of ancient behemoths such as Lehmann Brothers and Goldman Sachs, points to a systemic breakdown that may make the 1929 crisis look like a storm in a teacup.

I leave aside the larger question of what the agenda should be for the next conference on the systemic reorganisation of the institutions of global economic governance. The immediate question is: What should the leaders of the South be discussing in the corridors of the Doha meeting while negotiators are busy crafting a 'diplomatic text' containing half truths about the stark reality that the world faces today? Here are a few thoughts.

- The right to development of nations on their own terms must be the basis of financing for development. National projects should be supported only if they are rooted in local efforts in which all stakeholders are involved.
- Regional integration of countries in the South (and not free trade agreements between the North and the South) should be the basis of development cooperation. The primary institutions for protection against future market shocks and for credit for development should be regional. Regional banks in Asia, Africa and the Caribbean should carefully monitor the evolution of, for example, the Banco del Sur in Latin America.
- The BWIs are part of the problem, not part of the solution. In the interim, while new institutions of global economic governance are put in place, the BWIs must be made accountable to the Economic and Social Council (ECOSOC) of the UN.
- Democratisation and closer surveillance, oversight and regulation of international financial institutions (including the Basel Committee on Banking Supervision currently controlled by the Group of 10 – the G10), and private institutions of credit and capital flows (including hedge funds, private equity funds, and rating agencies) should be an essential feature of the new global financial architecture.

The dominant conceptualisation of the discourse on 'enhancing the coherence and consistency of the international monetary, financial and trading systems in support of development' (the subtitle of theme six of the Monterrey consensus) is seriously flawed. At present, the dominant theory and practice have made development a hostage to finance. The cart is before the horse. The correct realignment of the horse and cart would be a good start towards ensuring that finance serves development and not, as at present, the other way round. The current tendency of 'financialisation of development' has to be reversed into the 'developmentalisation of finance'. To do this, the Doha FfD conference must soon be followed by a new global conference on restructuring the architecture of global economic governance.

Ecuador's proposal on the financial crisis

16 November 2008

On 15 November 2008, at the invitation of President George W. Bush, a group of 20 countries (the G20) – selected by the president – met at the White House, and following three-and-half hours of discussion, issued a declaration on 'Financial Markets and the World Economy'. There was very little new or inspiring about the declaration. The G20 leaders made 'a commitment to free market principles, including the rule of law, respect for private property, open trade and investment, competitive markets, and efficient, effectively regulated financial systems.'

Their analysis of the 'Root causes of the current crisis' boiled down to blaming 'market participants' for seeking higher yields 'without appreciation of the risks'; in a world of 'increasingly complex and opaque financial products'; 'inconsistent and insufficiently coordinated macroeconomic policies'; and 'inadequate structural reforms' – all of which contributed to 'excesses and ultimately resulted in severe market disruption'.

Accordingly, the G20 leaders agreed to take some 'immediate steps' to stabilize the financial system, unfreeze credit markets, and ensure that the International Monetary Fund (IMF), the World Bank and the multilateral development banks (MDBs) had sufficient resources. Also, they agreed on five 'common principles': transparency, sound regulation, promoting financial integrity, international cooperation and reforming international financial institutions. These were followed by an action plan aimed at removing existing weaknesses in the accounting and disclosure procedures, credit rating agencies, pro-cyclical regulatory policies, etc; and the shortcomings of the Bretton Woods institutions including the IMF, the World Bank, the Basel Committee, and the Financial Stability Forum.

This is the sum total of the G20's unconvincing declaration. Cloaked in barely camouflaged ideological assumptions that are both historically and logically flawed, the declaration lacks both empirical correspondence to reality and theoretical depth.

At the Interactive Panel of the United Nations General Assembly on 31 October 2008, Pedro Páez Pérez, Ecuador's minister of economic policy coordination, presented an 'Agenda from the South' that is more realistic and pertinent for the South.[1] In contrast to the globalised integration model advocated by the G20, Pérez advocates a regional model, including 'decoupling from the dollar's crisis logic'. 'Today', he says, 'the commercial dependency (and intra-firm trade) with the North is sky high.' Pérez's observation is similar to my own in my recently published book, *Ending Aid Dependence*.

Pérez carefully goes through the political and technical arguments for creating regional monetary agreements (RMAs), including flexible regional bloc exchange rate regimes (ERR), and the creation of regional currencies. With these, the South can reduce 'the artificial need for dollars in the regional trade, financial markets, and therefore, the technical need for reserves through the deployment of intra-continental system of settlements'. These measures will converge towards 'a sense of regional identity, responsibility and community of interests ... and breaking out of the "prisoner's dilemma" of unilateral decision making.' In relation to Latin America, he advocates building on the 'New Regional Financial Architecture' agreed upon by the seven ministers of finance (Argentina, Bolivia, Brazil, Ecuador, Paraguay, Uruguay and Venezuela) in the Quito Declaration of 3 May 2008. He goes on to urge 'an international diplomatic campaign to launch, in parallel, similar accords in other regions of the world (Chiang Mai, Africa, Arab countries, etc.)'.

Pérez's proposal is in line with what we have been suggesting for some time in the *South Bulletin*. We have argued that it is imperative that the South decouples itself from the crisis-prone system of the North.

This is particularly urgent in the present phase of financialised capitalism when financial markets are privileged over production; when home mortgages, consumer spending, the commodity market, the oil market, the food market, etc, are all subject to asset securitisation and speculation in the uncontrollable futures market; and when profit maximisation by mostly Western banks and corporations, sometimes in collaboration with Southern large corporations, have disembowelled and weakened the resilience of smaller enterprises in the South and thrown them out of their domestic markets.

The sub-prime housing crisis which started with the US and then became globalised (to a greater degree in Europe than in Asia, Africa and Latin America) through inter-bank collateralised securities was not a product of 'severe market disruption' as the G20 declaration argues, but endemic to the present system of capitalism, part of its inner logic. In the 1990s British Prime Minister Margaret Thatcher coined the phrase 'There is No Alternative' (to neoliberalism), or TINA. In 2002, a new word entered the financial lexicography of housing mortgages – NINA (No Income, No Assets). People with neither income nor securities were provided mortgages by happily whistling bankers. These twin maids – TINA and NINA – have caused untold misery to the poor of both the North and the South.

This is only one side of the coin – the side of a globalised, financialised market of housing, stock and dot-com bubbles. The South must not forget the other side of the coin. In 1997 during the Asian financial crisis, Mahathir Mohamed, then prime minister of Malaysia, called for greater international control of the speculation of hedge funds such as George Soros' Quantum Fund. Northern 'experts' pronounced him 'mad'. But Mahathir saved his country from the prescriptions of the IMF, which brought the economies of Thailand, Indonesia and South Korea crashing down. As this was happening, curiously but not surprisingly, two hedge fund economists, Robert Merton and Myron Scholes, were awarded the Nobel Prize for their 'sterling work' in risk-free financial management. The Black-Scholes model was eagerly lapped up in university MBA curricula and commodity and currency exchanges. In 1998, tragedy struck. Long Term Capital Management (LTCM), of which Scholes and Merton were partners, crashed. At the time, LTCM had capital of $4.8 billion, a portfolio of $200 billion built from credit lines with all the major US and European banks, and derivatives with a notional value of $1,250 billion. Its CEO was the legendary hedge fund trader, John Meriwether, who when asked if he believed in efficient markets, replied, 'I make them efficient.'

In 1999, encouraged by US Federal Reserve Governor Alan Greenspan and US Treasury Secretary Robert Rubin, the Congress repealed the Glass-Steagall Act. This opened up a bonanza for US banks. They started snatching all kinds of assets from insurance companies, pension funds, finance houses, mortgage companies, etc. They also created 'innovative' financing instruments including collateral debt obligations (CDOs) and special purpose vehicles (SPVs) (see 'The global financial meltdown and lessons for the South' in this volume). What we are witnessing today is no ordinary 'cyclical crisis'. It is a deep-seated systemic crisis that cannot be resolved by a little patch-up work, fiscal injection and counter-cyclical measures suggested by the G20 declaration, which is inspired by President Bush's last minute effort to save 'free market' capitalism.

The South must not forget also that most of the present woes of many countries in the South stem from the conditionalities (such as the Structural Adjustment Programme) imposed on the countries that borrowed from the IMF and the World Bank. The IMF bailouts were not aimed at protecting the economies of the South. The objective, or at any rate the effect, of these was to bail out hard-pressed American financial and banking interests and to create conditions for the further control by American (and allied) capital of the national economies of the developing countries in distress. In other words, these developing countries were placed in distress through the debt burden, trade liberalisation and other conditionalities of donor funding – and then to get them out of the distress, the IMF moved in and cleared the way for American–European–Japanese capital to take over. This, at least, is what evidence showed on the ground. Even the London-based *The Economist* had to admit that IMF's Korea foray after the financial crisis of 1997/98 proved that the IMF had become an 'adjunct to US foreign policy'.[2] It went on to say that the US also had a 'big hand' in dictating IMF conditions for bailing out Mexico and Indonesia. In the IMF, *The Economist* concluded, it is 'politics in command'. Larry Summers, the intellectual power behind US economic foreign affairs, said: 'In some ways the IMF has done more in these past months to liberalise these economies and open their markets to US goods and services than has been achieved in rounds of trade negotiations in the region.'[3]

In a study undertaken by a group of researchers from both the North and the South in 2002–03, initially with the World Bank blessing (later the bank withdrew), found that the effects of Structural Adjustment Programmes (SAPs) on the economies of Bangladesh, Ecuador, El Salvador, Ghana, Hungary, Mexico, the Philippines, Uganda and Zimbabwe were 'disastrous'. It led to loss of policy space, privatisation of public assets (the reverse of what the Western governments are now doing in nationalising private banks and other assets), fiscal discipline (as opposed to fiscal leniency now adopted by Western governments when their own economies are in distress), deindustrialisation, unemployment, poverty, the collapse of social safety nets, food importation, and the creation of economic refugees and emigration.

The G20 declaration aims at restoring the legitimacy of the IMF by pumping money into it. At least it is an admission of the IMF's lack of legitimacy. However, no amount of replenishing the IMF's diminishing liquidity will restore its legitimacy in the eyes of the millions who have suffered under its disastrous policy prescriptions of the last nearly three decades. It is for these reasons that we must advise the countries of the South, especially the smaller and vulnerable ones, to challenge the simplistic analysis of the G20 declaration on the current crisis, its ill-conceived ideology of free market liberalism and its proposed remedies.

The Ecuadorian proposal[4] enunciated by Minister Pérez, on the other hand, has an alternative strategy for the South. 'As in other historical experiences,' says Pérez, 'the most vulnerable ones will end up paying for the excesses of others, unless a viable and technically well designed roadmap is created to defend their interests.' It is an outstanding example of innovative and practical thinking from the South. It is a doable strategy with a clear roadmap based on 'learning-by-doing'. It seeks to build confidence and trust through a 'collegial process' among countries in the three regions of the South (Asia, Africa and Latin America and the Caribbean). And it is 'oriented towards another kind of development and new relationships between states, capitalist firms and the heterogeneous spectrum of popular economies (medium, small and micro-enterprises, community and cooperative structures, etc).'

The Ecuadorian proposal deserves serious study and consideration by the leaders of the South, big and small. If the leaders of the seven countries of the South who went to Washington and after barely three-and-half hours of discussion of a precooked text endorsed the G20 declaration did so out of courtesy to the outgoing president of the US, then there is still hope. Diplomatic courtesy is part of the South's culture. That said, a serious debate is urgently needed in the South itself – between its political leaders, its academic and intellectual community, its civil society and above all, between all of these and the movements of the people on the ground who are at the receiving end of all ill-conceived policies done in their name. This is the democratic transparency that is needed, not the top–down financial and banking 'transparency' of the G20 declaration. People do matter.

Notes

1. Reproduced in *South Bulletin* (2008) no. 27, 16 November.
2. *The Economist* (1997), 13 December, p. 80.
3. *American Farmers: Their Stakes in Asia, Their Stake in IMF* (1998) Office of Public Affairs, US Treasury Department, Washington, DC.
4. Reproduced in *South Bulletin* (2008) no. 27, 16 November.

The decoupling imperative

1 November 2007

'Decoupling' is the idea that the economies of the industrialised and the developing countries are no longer closely related, and that a slowdown in the former can be offset by growth in the latter, especially in the BRIC countries – Brazil, Russia, India and China.

In its September 2007 report, for example, Goldman Sachs said that the world economy is decoupling from the US economy, and that BRIC are 'the key to global decoupling'. On 14 October 2007, the *Financial Times* carried an article saying that the London investors are buying into decoupling theory: big losses in property and banking is offset by boom in the oil, mining and IT stock because of emerging economies. Hence the UK stock market is bullish even when the UK economy itself is bearish. Growth in BRIC and their decoupling from the Western economies is good for the UK. On the other hand, Wolfgang Munchau, associate editor of the *Financial Times*, writing on 16 April 2007, says that he does not support this theory: the US consumer market is simply too important for other countries to ignore.

There are thus two aspects to this debate. One is whether it is empirically true to say that the bigger countries of the South are indeed 'decoupling' from Western economy. And the second is whether it is a good thing.

Leaving aside the empirical issue for now, on the prescriptive issue we argue that it is indeed imperative that the developing countries strive to decouple (or what we prefer to call 'selectively disengage') from Western economies. They may seek markets in the West, but they must reduce their dependence on them and seek to develop markets in the South. This is already happening. Silvia Liu of Merrill Lynch says that Asian dependence on the US consumer market has declined dramatically from 8 per cent of total exports in 2001 to 6 per cent in 2006. An increasing share of global trade is now between the countries of the South. Growth in China and India partly accounts for the current boom in certain commodities, especially oil and minerals.

Trade, in goods and services, is only one aspect of globalisation. Its more risky aspect is the Western financial system, its complete dependence on the US dollar, and the unpredictability and eccentricities of US speculative markets. We have already witnessed how the sub-prime debacle, over junk mortgages sold to poorly rated buyers in the US, spread to Europe and threw, for example, the UK banking system into a spin. Luckily for Asia, it is sufficiently 'decoupled' from the US not to suffer the same fate as it did in the late 1990s following Western speculators' run on the Thai currency. As a caution, one must add, however, that the extent of Asian involvement in the sub-prime crisis through the collateralised debt obligations is still unknown. (CDOs are complex financial tools that securitise debts that are then sold globally.)

Nonetheless, the sub-prime crisis shows that it is imperative for the South, above all, to decouple or 'selectively disengage' from the contagious effects of Western financial and speculative markets. These and asset pricing mechanisms are even more risky for the South than terms of trade.

Decoupling, if it has not happened, is now an economic and political imperative for the South.

Banco del Sur – another step towards decoupling

16 November 2007

After much speculation and some hostile coverage in the Western media the Banco del Sur – the Bank of the South (BdS) – is to be launched on 5 December 2007. It was thought that close US allies – Mexico, Colombia, Peru and Central America – might oppose its formation. This may have been mere wishful thinking, as most of South America is now on board.

Because the initiative came from President Chavez, some doubted if the new bank would not simply become his political instrument. Paradoxically, this must be on account of the experience with the IMF. It is well known that the IMF cannot move without a mandate from the United States. Presently its largest lending goes to Turkey and Pakistan, and this is not surprising. However, unlike the IMF whose governance is highly undemocratic, the BdS governance is based on the principle of *one country one vote.*

Naturally, there are still many questions to be settled, for example, lending policies and rules, who may borrow and at what terms, and whether BdS should act strictly as a development bank, or whether, like the IMF, it should also act as a bank of last resort for countries in balance of payments difficulties. These are weighty policy and operational matters. With time, they will no doubt be resolved and tested on the ground. Of course, mistakes will be made in the early years, but hopefully, a robust system will emerge in the not too distant future. After all, what BdS is attempting to do has never been tried. It is, indeed, quite revolutionary in its ambition and far-reaching in its potential impact on the global financial architecture.

If the BdS grows to its potential, Latin American countries will be freed from the conditionalities of the IMF, the World Bank and the Inter-American Development Bank, which chained their economies to the failed macroeconomic policies of the Bretton Woods institutions. 'Decoupling' from the US-led global economic hegemony has so far only been an idea, and applied mostly in the cases of China, India and Brazil. But now 'decoupling' the whole of Latin America from volatilities of the Western credit system is a vision in the realm of reality.

There are, however, certain matters that must engage the new bank in the interest of ensuring that it really does serve as a genuine development bank.

First, the bank must promote a new strategy of development, one that promotes innovation, production and employment, and, above all, one that serves the needs of the poor rather than accumulation by the rich.

Second, the new Bank should focus on the regional economic integration of Latin America and the Caribbean states (if they should eventually join it). There are excellent banks in the continent that serve national priorities. Brazil's National Bank of Economic and Social Development (BNDES) alone lends $30 billion annually, four times more than the $7 billion subscribed to the new BdS. There is Corporacion Andino de Fomento (CAF), the largest lender to the five Andean countries. They will no doubt continue their excellent work. But BdS needs to provide financial muscle to the integration of the continent as a strong regional economic bloc. (The IDB presently invests only 2 per cent on regional integration – clearly not one its priorities.)

Third, the bank must move away from the Basel regulatory system which works to the detriment of development. Development lending is often a high-risk operation. The minimum capital requirement of Basel unduly leverages attractiveness of 'low-risk' to 'higher-risk' financing. Basel regulatory arbitrage favours low-risk lending and adds cost to development lending, which is one reason for scarcity of development capital in the South. Basel II's 'Internal Ratings-Based Approach' creates even more bias against risk and cost of borrowing. The new bank must, of course, be prudent in its lending, but it needs to balance the needs of development with the returns to capital for the lenders of capital. It must operate as a genuine bank for the people.

A new geopolitical double paradox stalks the world

16 February 2008

The gap between the rich and the poor between and within nations continues to grow. This has been the defining characteristic of the last 40 years of 'development', underscored by several reports from intergovernmental organisations (such as the World Bank and the United Nations Conference on Trade and Development – UNCTAD) as well as from non-governmental ones (such as Oxfam and the World Council of Churches). This phenomenon continues unabated.

But now there is a new geopolitical double paradox that stalks the world. One aspect of this double paradox has to do with the relation between some increasingly wealthy countries in the South and the older wealthy countries of the North. Wealth is still very unevenly distributed, with the North still holding the vast amount of historically accumulated assets. However, countries like China, India and Brazil (because of their large domestic markets and increased competitiveness in the export markets), and countries such as those in the Gulf (because of the exorbitant escalation of oil prices in recent years), are accumulating enormous wealth. These *nouveau riche* nations now have enough wealth not only to buy off some of the major assets owned by northern corporations, but also to recapitalise northern private equity firms and banks in the throes of a deepening credit squeeze. This is one aspect of the paradox. The implications of this paradox have not been fully understood let alone analysed.

But there is yet another aspect of this new geopolitical paradox. Among the nations of the South, there is an increasing divide between the newly enriched large nations and the vast bulk of the nations of the South (more than two-thirds of the total) that are coming under the more entrenched domination and control of the older countries of the North. There is much talk about the increasing South–South trade and investment flows, and yes, there is enough empirical data to show this. But, at the same time, there are many countries in the South whose structural ties with the Northern countries are further entrenched and deepened. Even as South–South trade and investment is increasing, the underlying structures, institutions and rules of trade and investments are defined not by the South–South linkages, but by the older North–South former colonial linkages. This, indeed, is an odd paradox.

Let us look at this more closely. Take the agreements, for example, that are being concluded between the European Union and the African, Caribbean and Pacific (ACP) countries, and the bilateral trade and investment agreements being negotiated between the older countries of the North and the poorer countries of the South (between, for example, the United States and the Central American countries). These relations are setting the norms and rules by which these countries become further tied to the older wealthier countries of the North, which, ironically, are themselves in the throes of an economic and financial crisis. Even as the relatively few wealthy countries of the South are partially 'decoupling' from the North, the majority of their poorer sister nations are 'recoupling' with the North. Just as some of the bigger countries in the South are getting wealthier, their poorer brethren in the South are getting neocolonised.

Is there a connection between the two aspects of this double paradox? Is it the case that just as the older richer nations of the world are losing out, relatively speaking, to some of the new richer nations of the South, those in the North have no choice but to further control whatever is left of the former colonies and dependencies of the South? Is the entrenchment of what are evidently neocolonial ties with the poorer countries of the South – mostly in Africa, the poorer nations in Latin America and Asia, and the Caribbean and the Pacific – one of the ways in which the older countries in the North can maintain their competitiveness against the small number of the nouveau riche nations of the South?

Plenoxia – the desire to have more and more, in this case of wealth – has seized the psychology of the newly wealthy in the rich countries of the South as well as the rich in the older countries of the North. Is its one consequence the forced anorexia of the poorer nations, and worse, the poorest people within the poor nations?

The Non-Aligned Movement and the collapse of the Doha round

1 August 2008

In the week ending July 2008, Geneva and Teheran sent two parallel signals to the world. In Geneva the Doha round of trade negotiations, conducted within the multilateral framework of the World Trade Organisation (WTO), collapsed. In Teheran the Non-Aligned Movement (NAM) re-emerged, invigorated by the collective action of its 118 member states. What accounted for the failure of one and the success of the other?

Two global political-economic undercurrents have surfaced that may explain this dual phenomenon. The first is the futile attempt by the power holders of the old order to sustain that order, including an outdated and unfair trading regime. The second is the countervailing power emerging in the South that is challenging the old order. The world is going through a period of transition from one order to another. The new order is still in the making, its essential features are in the twilight zone and are symbolised by the actions of the WTO and NAM.

The WTO is a global trading and negotiating body where economic power asymmetries are played out during this transition period. The negotiated texts of the WTO are binding, backed by the power of sanctions. Sanctions are an instrument more likely to be used by the developed than the developing countries. The developed countries (with the help of the WTO secretariat) are trying to use the present power asymmetry to extract the most they can from the developing countries, especially from the bigger countries such as Brazil, China, India and South Africa. The latter, in turn, are seeking maximum market access in the older countries of the North (US and EU), while protecting the home front. The smaller players (especially the least developed countries) are asked to stand aside while the 'big boys' are battling it out in semi-closed, semitransparent meetings. Both sides (the old big guys and the new big guys) are fighting principally for their own national interests. This is the age-old mercantilist battle. However, these days it is done in the name of 'development'. Development is the current ideological and legitimising norm, but it has a flexible definition, and the two sides seek to provide their own definition and methodology for achieving it.

This time around, in Geneva, the new big guys appear to be winning. China, which normally plays a low-key role at the WTO, decided to throw its weight behind the countries of the South. It has correctly read the signs of growing protectionism in the US and the European Union. The US and the EU are reluctant to change their regime of subsidies (especially in agriculture) unless they get substantial concessions from the South in manufacturing (the so-called Non-Agricultural Market Access neogtiations) and services. But they are demanding too much. If granted, these concessions have the potential not only to destroy the manufacturing and services sectors in the big countries of the South, but they will also foreclose any possibility of developing these sectors in the smaller countries. Here is where the South gets the material and ideological basis of their unity. China's trading, investment and even political future lies with the other developing countries. These include not only the big countries such as India and Brazil, but also smaller ones in Africa, Asia and Latin America.

Thus, despite many differences, even contradictions, among the countries of the South arising out of their different histories, geopolitical circumstances and varying levels of development, there is a greater sense of self-confidence and unity of purpose in the South than ever before. This is what explains the two trajectories of WTO and NAM. This new geopolitical configuration brought down the North-imposed multilateral trading system of the WTO in Geneva, and rejuvenated NAM in Teheran. China is not a member of NAM, but it is there in spirit with its newly acquired wealth and influence.

To this economic dimension must be added a political one. The developed countries have become increasingly intrusive in the internal affairs of the countries of the South in the name of human rights, the rule of law and democratic governance (as defined by the West). This is widely resented by the countries of the South. The South values these norms, although admittedly many of them are having difficulties in realising these norms in their countries. But they do not like Western intrusion; they want to develop their own norms and institutions.

Among other things, the NAM ministerial meeting in Teheran,

in a clear message to the dominant powers, stated the following: 'Refrain from recognising, adopting or implementing extra-territorial or unilateral coercive measures or laws, including unilateral economic sanctions, other intimidating measures, and arbitrary travel restrictions that seek to exert pressure on Non-Aligned countries – threatening their sovereignty and independence, and their freedom of trade and investment – and prevent them from exercising their right to decide, by their own free will, their own political, economic and social systems...[and] request States applying these measures or laws to revoke them fully and immediately.'

The NAM document named and honoured the visionary founding fathers of the movement – President Kwame Nkrumah of Ghana, President Achmad Sukarno of Indonesia, President Gamal Abdul Nasser of the United Arab Republic (Egypt), President Josip Broz Tito of Yugoslavia and Prime Minister Jawarharlal Nehru of India. It recorded that the movement played a key role in the process of decolonisation, deracialisation and demilitarisation of international society, especially their manifestations in the former colonies in the South. Those, we must add, are still ongoing battles at the global level.

Some (both in the North and the South) have argued that with the end of the cold war, the non-alignment movement has lost its raison d'être. Teheran (and before that Havana, Kuala-Lumpur and Durban where the preceding meetings of NAM were held) showed that far from dying, NAM has revived itself. The G77, China and NAM set up a Joint Coordinating Committee (JCC) in New York in 1994 with the objective of pursuing developing countries' common goals and harmonising and coordinating their activities. In 1996, it put in place a system of work called the *Cartegena Document on Methodology of the Movement*. A troika of the past, present and future elected chairmen, represented by their ambassadors in New York, serve as a kind of secretariat and coordinating body of NAM.

The South Centre works closely with the G77, NAM and the JCC. The Centre provides independent expert advice based on rigorous research and analysis to the G77 and NAM. The South Centre acts like a kind of midwife in this transition period where the old order is slowly dying and the new one is yet to be born.

2

Restructuring global governance

Introduction

This chapter brings together the editorials that sought to address questions and issues arising out of what in essence are the politics of global governance. In the introduction to the last chapter a question was raised: Should not the economic relationship between countries of the South (South–South relations) be built on a different model from the greed and profit-driven model of North–South relations? A parallel issue arises at the level of political governance. Should not the political relationship between countries of the South be built on a different model from the top–down, patronising and interfering model of North–South relations? The North argues that under certain circumstances – for example, the violation of human rights or of property rights in the South; the threat to security caused by terrorism or by the phenomenon of 'failed states'; and the non-fulfilment of the conditions of aid or capital investment – they have the right to intervene in the internal affairs of the countries of the South. Often, they intervene directly but, equally often, they do so through the instruments of global governance, such as the United Nations, the Bretton Woods institutions and the Organisation of Economic Cooperation and Development (OECD). The question is: To what extent can this be the model for global governance? The editorials in this chapter do not address all these issues. However, the perspective they provide can form the basis for some new thinking on this important matter.

In 'Good governance, colonial guilt and contemporary challenges', an editorial that was written during the riots in Kenya following the controversial elections in December 2007, some of these issues are partially addressed. Following a serious crisis of governance in Kenya, the country witnessed unprecedented violence that ominously looked like ethnic cleansing. Fortunately, a negotiated deal between the rival political forces was concluded with the timely intervention of the heads of states of some of the neighbouring countries led by Kofi Annan. What is significant about this *regional form of mediation* is that it neutralised direct or indirect intervention by the former colonial and imperial powers, who might have intervened with the ostensible objective of restoring 'good governance', but with the primary intention of advancing their own interests. This is part of the present tragedy of Zimbabwe. Deeper thinking shows that the 'governance crises' in Zimbabwe or Kenya, or for that matter in most conflict situations in the South (Somalia, Darfur, Sri Lanka, Pakistan, Palestine, Venezuela and Bolivia), are a throwback from colonial history and to the ethnic and class structure that evolved during and after the colonial period. In such conflict situations, the imperial powers continue to have vested interests; they continue to try to influence the resolution of the conflicts in order, primarily, to serve their imperial or colonial settler interests. The editorial concludes that regional mediation can help, as the example of Kenya shows. However, the underlying causes and the difficult task of 'nation-building' will ultimately have to be addressed by the people and political leadership of the country. The challenge for the political leadership in Africa, as in the rest of the South, is to persist in the 'National Project': the challenge of building viable nations out of the fragmented and divided societies left behind by the colonial period.

In this context, it is important to recognise the role of civil society. Nation-building is too serious a matter to be left to governments or the politicians alone. Too often, with their eyes on foreign aid and foreign capital, governments in the South allow national policies to be subjected to the dictates of the larger institutions of global economic governance, such as the International Monetary Fund (IMF), the World Bank and the Organisation of Economic Cooperation and Development (OECD). In 'The role of civil society in national space', we argue that it is the responsibility of the people and of civil society to hold their governments to account and to ensure that national policy space is not auctioned off in the market place of aid and capital. For the last 30 years the IMF–World Bank have pushed the strategies of their Structural Adjustment Programmes (SAPs) and the Poverty Reduction Strategy Papers (PRSPs), which have been a tragedy for the poorer countries of the South. The editorial asks: Do the civil society organisations (CSOs) of the South wish to repeat the tragedy for the next 30 years by surrendering their national democratic space to the donors, the OECD, the IMF and the World Bank, over whom they have no control?

The one institution of global governance is the G7/8, consisting of countries of the North that have arrogated to themselves the mandate to govern the rest of the world. In 'The G8 has no legitimacy – it should dissolve itself' we examine the credibility of the G8 as an institution of global governances. It has the power of the mighty, but it does not have the voice of the people. That shrewd combination of power plus voice that the founders of the United Nations correctly forged in the world body is lacking in the G8. The G8 is a self-selected club of the rich and powerful. Nobody ever gave it the mandate or authority to decide on matters of the economy, climate change or security, or to impose sanctions on states that do not bend to their will. The editorial, written after the G8 summit in Hokkaido in July 2008, criticised the decisions taken by the G8, including on climate change and Zimbabwe. It argues that this self-selected body has no legitimacy whatsoever and should therefore dissolve itself. The big powers should surrender their will to the wider accountability system of the United Nations.

The UN is the embodiment of multilateralism, which is a good thing, but it comes with a price. Any multilaterally agreed text – whether it is within the UN framework or within the framework of, for example, peace negotiations – has to be negotiated between states. Here, power, resources and access to knowledge are significant factors that influence the outcome of the negotiations. The resultant outcomes are what might be called 'diplomatic truths', as opposed to what we call 'existential truths'. This is the theme of the editorial 'UNCTAD XII: negotiating diplomatic truths', written on the eve of the 12th conference of the United Nations Conference on Trade and Development. It argues that the 'negotiated' compromises of truth camouflages huge differences on political and policy issues that obscure the 'reality' on the ground. For example, the negotiated or diplomatic truth about globalisation is a compromise between those who view it as an opportunity and those who view it as a challenge. It is an interim truth about a very complex reality on the ground. It is for this reason that there is never a definitive definition of globalisation in the diplomatic discourse. There cannot be one. However, despite its interim and negotiated character, diplomatic truth is not unreal, it is only a different kind of reality. The bottom line is that those that have more power will exact a desired outcome from those that are weak and vulnerable. Ultimately, however, if the diplomatic truths are totally at variance with the existential reality, then those truths are unenforceable, as has been happening with the power-enforced agreements on Palestine, or what could happen with the European Union-enforced economic partnership agreements (EPAs).

Notwithstanding this underlying weakness in the institutions of the UN, it is still the most credible multilateral institution we have. It is generally known that many countries in the West, and in particular the United States and the United Kingdom, seek to weaken the UN. They prefer to take matters outside the UN system, whether these deal with security, development or climate change. They try to co-opt selected leaders from the South to join institutions created by them (like the G7/8 did by inviting five bigger countries from the South to their Hokkaido meeting) rather than bring matters to the open forums of the UN system. But this ploy, while self-serving in the short run, is also self-defeating. This is the theme of 'Why strengthening UNCTAD is also in the interest of the North'.

This is the context that provides the theme of the editorial 'South expectations of the Development Cooperation Forum'. The Development Cooperation Forum (DCF) was an outcome of the World Summit in 2005 in an attempt to strengthen the Economic and Social Council (ECOSOC) of the UN. It was also an implied critique of the Western dominated 'development' agencies such as the Development Assistance Committee (DAC) of the Organisation of Economic Cooperation and Development (OECD), which is largely a club of the rich former colonial and imperial powers, and which suffers from a democratic and governance deficit. The primary objective of the DCF was to strengthen the link between the normative and operational work of the UN on matters related to development. However, this is not happening. Imperial interests do not give in easily. Having failed to provide legitimacy to the DAC, the OECD countries have effectively seized the DCF so that they can import their own agenda and perspectives into the forum, in particular the equation that aid equals development. The executive director of the South Centre is a member of the advisory group of the DCF, but he has been effectively marginalised by the manipulations of the donors within the UN bureaucracy. However, on the basis of research undertaken in Geneva and in four research centres (in Brazil, China, India and South Africa) the South Centre identified the South's expectations of the DCF and the editorial attempts to summarise these.

The World Trade Organisation (WTO) is another such institution of global governance. In 'A case for radical reform of the World Trade Organisation' we analyse how Geneva provides the detached ambience in which diplomats from the South and the North negotiate on matters from trade to intellectual property regimes, and from disarmament to human rights. Geneva throws a comfortable veil over proceedings, making them aloof from the real world. The negotiations feel abstracted from the reality of power politics. Geneva is a synthetic, sanitised place. In such an environment, thinking becomes universalised and idealised abstractions from reality. And when it comes to trade negotiations within the subliminal waterfront façade of the WTO, mathematical formalism, an abstruse numbers game, takes over in ever-repeating incantations of the same insipid formulae. Coefficients and percentages parody life. It is in this surrealist atmosphere that the Doha round, based on the now clearly falsified ideology that free trade is good for all, has become stuck. The existential reality of life has negated the diplomatic reality of trade negotiations. The WTO needs to be radically reformed and adjusted to the harsh reality out there. The WTO is about the only organisation (besides the Security Council of the United Nations) that has teeth. The WTO can bite. This – the enforcement pillar of the WTO – needs to be critically reviewed. Has it really brought gains of development for the global poor? Why was the WTO given teeth in the first place, while its predecessor, the GATT, had none? This is even more critical in the present conjuncture when its second pillar – the ideological pillar – is now fully discredited. The vacuous basis of its underlying premises has been amply exposed in the financial meltdown of the casino economy as well as by the historical experiences of the South itself.

Finally, to come to the last editorial in this chapter, the South recognises the role that the United States can play in the global arena. In 'A perspective on the American presidential elections', written while Obama and Clinton were still campaigning for the Democratic nomination, we argue that given that the US has such a powerful influence in world affairs, which affects the lives of ordinary people everywhere, it is permissible to express an opinion on what kind of US leader is right from a global perspective. Sadly, however, the American elections are very parochial. That the American voters put the national and domestic interests of America up front in their choice of president is understandable. Nonetheless, an enlightened American voter should define national interest broadly enough to include a global perspective.

Unfortunately, that perspective is obsessively and compulsively focused on a vision of national security and well-being that is narrowly defined. It is a perspective that has jeopardised the lives and well-being of ordinary people in the rest of the world, the safety and sustainability of the natural environment – a milieu that knows no electoral boundaries – and the stability of the global financial system. The American system of production and consumption has allowed its citizens to consume more than they produce, which translates into trillions of dollars that pour from mainly the global South – a form of South subsidy for America's self-indulgent lifestyle.

The monopolisation and commercialisation of knowledge by private corporations for profit in the US, as in the EU, is the most critical obstacle to the development of the South. Private appropriation of public knowledge is indefensible under any political system that seeks moral legitimacy, as any global power must. Unfortunately, the American electorate and education system are not open enough to allow these kinds of issues to enter into the debate around the election of their president. The editorial argues that the new leadership of the United States must face up to its responsibility towards global citizenry. We hope that President Obama's background and education will help him overcome these real barriers to true democracy and global awareness in the US.

Good governance, colonial guilt and contemporary challenges

1 March 2008

The developing countries are being encouraged to adopt good governance and investment reforms as a way of improving the investment climate and efficiency. At one level, this prescription is only common sense. Who can doubt the importance of good governance, or of efficiency in the use of capital, or of improving the investment climate?

However, matters are not as simple as they appear at first sight. Lack of clarity on this matter leads to simplistic policy prescriptions, or illusory 'capacity building' projects in the vain hope that these will lead to good governance and an improvement in the climate for investments. A couple of examples may help illustrate the point

Take Kenya, for example. After over four decades of independence and a relatively favourable climate for investment and development, the country has erupted into a state of violence and a crisis of governance. The much-heralded constitutional reforms had become bogged down in controversy over power sharing. The post-independence project of nation-building was in peril. As we go to press, it is a relief to learn that outside mediation efforts led by Kofi Annan have finally succeeded in breaking the power and constitutional logjam. But there are still deeper issues that need to be addressed. These relate to poverty, land distribution and the evolving ethnic and class nature of society, the origins of which go back to the colonial period. External mediation can help pave the way, but the underlying causes and the difficult task of nation-building will have to be ultimately addressed by the people and political leadership of the country.

Take the war in Darfur as another example. The earlier civil war in the South of the Sudan had both ethnic and religious dimensions. In Darfur, the main fault lines appear to be ethnic and tribal. The conflict, however, has become internationalised. Some in the West have described it as 'genocide'. The West has also charged that China is not doing enough to put pressure on the government of the Sudan and of 'complicity' by default.

Recently, Steven Spielberg, the Oscar-winning American director, announced that he was quitting the Olympic Games' opening ceremonies to protest against Beijing's alleged support for the Sudanese government. But again, matters are not as simple as they appear. The whole of that region, including the Sudan, Somalia, Ethiopia, Eritrea, Kenya and the Great Lakes region, has suffered from its colonial past and post-colonial traumas resulting from scarcity of water for livestock, land shortages and land grabbing, drought and desertification, and above all, the breakdown of all structures of governance and conflict resolution that had existed in the pre-colonial past. This is not to condone what is happening in Darfur, nor to excuse the current political leadership from responsibility for the ongoing tragedy.

Nonetheless, in all the talk about good governance and reforming the investment climate, there is no escaping the fact that there are serious and deeply embedded issues relating to creating governance structures and that these remain a challenge. The structures created during the colonial period not only took advantage of the racial, ethnic and religious divisions of the colonised societies in a policy of 'divide and rule', but reinforced these divisions in the structures of governance left behind at independence. What is even more to the point is that the policy of divide and rule continues unabated to this day. Anybody who is closely monitoring the current negotiations between the European Union and the African, Caribbean and Pacific (ACP) countries would be left in no doubt about the validity of this statement.

The battle lines of the future in Africa are drawn in its oil wells, minerals and natural resources. These are resources the West needs. These are also the resources China and India need. In a new scramble for Africa's resources, the challenge lies with the current political leadership in Africa and in the bigger countries of the South, including China, India and Brazil, who have in their own history suffered colonial plunder. The talk about a good investment climate and good governance is naïve, and even rhetorical, if these are perceived as projects that can be fixed with a bit of money and technical assistance. *What is needed is a new model of relationship between the developed and the less developed countries.*

The more developed countries among the South must provide an alternative model for relating to the less developed ones, and not mimic those of the 19th century colonial period. Ultimately, however, it is the leadership in the less developed countries that must take the burden and responsibility of creating these relationships. There are some good examples in Africa of wise political leadership that is healing the wounds of the past and creating indigenously accountable structures of governance. But there are others that are failing to do so. The challenge of the political leadership in Africa, above all, but also in the rest of the South, is to persist in the national project, the challenge of building viable nations out of the fragmented and divided societies left behind in the wake of the colonial period.

The G8 has no legitimacy – it should dissolve itself

16 July 2008

Legitimacy is a philosophical–political concept. It is also an ethical concept. In Western philosophy a distinction is sometimes made between legality and legitimacy. Before the dawn of liberal democracy in the West, the will of the sovereign monarch constituted the legal order. Their decision was final. The French Revolution changed that. Henceforth, only the will of the people, expressed through representative institutions or directly by referendum, conferred legitimacy to the legal order. Last week, for example, the people of Ireland decided by referendum that contrary to the will of their government, they did not want to surrender their sovereignty to some supranational body called the European Union. This did not please many outsiders, but it nonetheless made the legitimacy of the Lisbon Treaty questionable. In June 2005, the peoples of France and the Netherlands had also decided to reject the proposed European constitution. Most governments in Europe are therefore not keen to test the political will of their people on the European constitution.

Nonetheless, what the Irish vote showed was that the democratically expressed will of the people is the ultimate test of the legitimacy of any institution that seeks to make decisions on behalf of the people.

Of course, the international domain is different from the national. There is no Parliament of the World's People, at least not yet. Here states represent their nationals in international discourse and negotiations. The nearest we have to a people's assembly is the United Nations. The UN, however, is a cleverly devised global body based on an adroit balance between power (the Security Council with big power veto) and the voice of the people (the General Assembly, where this voice is presumably articulated through governments). This is the UN's ultimate legitimacy test: Does it properly balance the power of the mighty with the voice of the world's people?

Fifty years after its formation, the General Assembly has more or less maintained its representative character. It has, for example, absorbed all the 'new nations' arising out of a colonial past and given them an equal voice in the assembly. It still enjoys some legitimacy. However, the Security Council has lost its legitimacy; it no longer reflects the new reality of power. The exercise of a 'triple veto' by the three Western nations of the United States, the United Kingdom and France while excluding countries such as India and Brazil from the citadels of power does not make sense any longer. Nonetheless, as long as the Security Council does not reform, it is the body that decides, for example, whether or not the internal situation in Zimbabwe constitutes a 'threat to international security' under Chapter VII of the Charter. The UN is a rule-based institution, even if the rules are now applied by an anachronistic Security Council.

The G8, on the other hand, has no legitimacy whatsoever. It has the power of the mighty, but it does not have the voice of the people. That shrewd combination of power plus voice that the founders of the UN correctly forged in the world body is lacking in the G8. The G8 is a self-selected club of the rich and powerful. Nobody ever gave it the mandate or authority to decide on matters of economy, climate change and security, nor to impose sanctions on states that do not bend to their will. The G8 summit that met in the island of Hokkaido in Japan sat in judgment over the democratic credentials of the government of Zimbabwe, but itself had no legitimacy. The G8 had no choice but to bring the matter to the Security Council of the UN where the West lost the vote because China and Russia vetoed it and South Africa opposed the West. The Western countries are understandably frustrated, but have only themselves to blame. They continue to harbour the illusion that their self-created G8 has legitimacy.

It is not that they are not conscious of their weakness, but illusions die hard. At the Heiligendamm G8 meeting last year, they tried to include the big five of the South to provide it with a veneer of legitimacy – the so-called Heiligendamm Process – but they failed. And they failed again in Hokkaido. The G8 is no longer even the seat of the powerful. It is a club of the six richest Western countries – France, Germany, Italy, the United Kingdom, the United States and Canada, plus one rich Asian country (Japan) and 'nearly rich' Russia, a former Communist country that was 'admitted' in 1998, but still sits, uncomfortably, in the margins of G7. This is the de facto international community one often hears or reads about. This so-called international community has no legitimacy.

As the immediate former president of Tanzania, Benjamin W. Mkapa, and chairman of the South Centre, said in addressing the InterAction Council (a grouping of former heads of state and government from the four continents) at its annual meeting in Sweden last week, 'The so-called "will of the international community" is no more than the will of the "coalition of the willing" at any one time.'

As it turned out, the so-called G5 developing nations (Brazil, China, India, Mexico and South Africa) that were invited to the Hokkaido Summit 'as observers' declared that they had no particular appetite for a pre-cooked dinner in which they had no hand in preparing. They constituted themselves into the coalition of the unwilling, and issued their own political declaration. On the matter of climate change, for example, while the European countries were celebrating that they were able 'to get the US on board' to any target at all (even one that mentions 50 per cent by 2020 without stating what base year they were referring to), the G5 leaders had a more concrete and, following Kyoto and Bali, a legally binding formulation. They placed performance targets on the developed countries, calling for quantified emission targets for these countries under the Kyoto Protocol after 2012, 'of at least 25–40 per cent below 1990 levels by 2020 and by 2050, by between 80 and 95 per cent below those levels, with comparability of efforts among them'.

Furthermore, the G5 leaders called for a strengthened scheme for technology transfer and 'a comprehensive review of the intellectual property rights regime for such technologies in order to strike an adequate balance between reward for innovators and the global public good.' The G8 missed out on the wisdom of the voice of the South by shortsightedly presuming to co-opt the big five to a preordained agenda. They thought that if they finally got the US on board on climate change, the G5 would also rejoice. They were creating grounds for their own disappointment. They thought that if they put the president of South Africa in a corner in Hokkaido and pressed him to give the G8 'the legitimacy it lacked' to impose sanctions on Zimbabwe, they would be able to reverse the decision of the African Union (AU), taken the previous week at Sharm al Shaikh. They did not realise that despite its weaknesses the AU has more legitimacy than the G8.

There was at least one honest G8 leader. At a press conference, President Nicolas Sarkozy of France said it was 'unreasonable to seek to tackle global issues without India, China, a country from South America, one from Africa and even an Arab country.' But even Sarkozy fell short of his worthy nation's revolutionary democratic credentials. For even if a 'representative nation' from each of these regions were to become members of this exclusive club, it would not provide the new body (G15, or G20, or even G30) the legitimacy it would need to presume to take a decision on behalf of the international community.

What is needed is a radical reform of the Security Council of the UN, not a patch-up job of the G8 that should, by now, dissolve itself. It does not constitute 'the international community' that it thinks it does.

UNCTAD XII: negotiating diplomatic truths

1 April 2008

Multilateralism comes with the price that any text within the UN framework, such as the text that will be negotiated at UNCTAD XII, has to be negotiated between member states. Here, power, resources and access to knowledge are significant factors that influence the outcome of negotiations. Agreed principles such as 'special and differential treatment' for least developed countries (LDCs) in trade negotiations and 'common and differentiated responsibilities' in climate change negotiations are indeed important, and in the hands of clever negotiators, they can change the outcome of negotiations, or provide subtle nuances. But, on balance, it is the underlying power structures (and this includes not only political and economic power but also power over knowledge and knowledge production) that determine the outcome of the negotiations. The resultant outcomes are what may be called 'diplomatic truths'.

Diplomatic truths, in other words, are truths as negotiated between states in the global system of asymmetrically positioned power relationships. These truths may have little or only partial correspondence with existential truths about reality on the ground. Those who have to make a living out of their impoverished resources may wonder in awe at the diplomatic truths negotiated in their name by their representatives in multilateral forums. Existential and diplomatic truths are two different things.

Take the Millennium Development Goals (MDGs), for example. The MDGs were a negotiated compromise text. They are not exactly what the G77 developing countries wanted. They do not address the root causes of underdevelopment in many countries of the global South. They are merely statistical representation of targets that the international community hopes to achieve by the year 2015 in respect of a selected number of what may be called 'public social goods'. They are the promise of hope over despair.

However, in order to vindicate the diplomatic reality of the MDGs, there are frequent official reports that these targets are being fulfilled, or where they are not, the reports become an argument for trying to do better, to raise more funds, for example. And yet the reality on the ground may be very different from official reports. For example, according to the Basic Capabilities Index (BCI) published by Social Watch on 7 June 2007, the target of universal access to a minimum set of social services, at the current rate of progress, will be achieved in sub-Saharan Africa only in 2108. This means a delay of almost a century. Furthermore, according to a recent report by UNICEF, of the 62 countries making no progress or insufficient progress towards the MDG on child survival, nearly 75 per cent are in Africa. In Southern Africa, for example, because of AIDS infections, tuberculosis, malaria and under-nutrition, the incidence of infant and under-five mortality has actually increased.

Take a more abstract example, that of the debate about globalisation. In multilateral diplomatic forums (e.g. UNCTAD or WTO), it is defined in the course of negotiations between contending political forces in a particular context. Africans might argue that they have not seen many benefits of globalisation, that all they have seen are its negative consequences. They would present it as a challenge. The developed countries might argue, on the other hand, that much of the benefits of globalisation have not permeated Africa because of internal governance problems in Africa, the alleged corruption of its leaders, and the failure to create conditions for investments to flow. Globalisation, they would argue, has not really been given a chance. Hence, while recognising that it might be a challenge, they would argue that it is also an opportunity, one that Africans may not have adequately seized. The negotiated or diplomatic truth about globalisation is thus a compromise between these two views; it is then presented as both an opportunity and a challenge, to satisfy the two interlocutors. However, this compromise camouflages huge differences on political and policy issues that obscure the reality on the ground. It is an interim truth, a negotiated truth about a very complex reality on the ground. It is for this reason that there is never a definitive definition of globalisation in the diplomatic discourse. There cannot be one.

Nonetheless – and this is the point of this editorial – despite its interim and negotiated character, diplomatic truth is not unreal. It is only a different kind of reality; it is reality based on power relationships. Principles and values are part of the power relationships and to some extent mitigate the influence of naked power, but the bottom line is that those that have more power will exact a desired outcome from those that are weak and vulnerable, as the present negotiations on Economic Partnership Agreements (EPAs) between the European Union and the African, Caribbean and Pacific (ACP) countries well illustrate.

Nonetheless, power in international relations is a reality. Equally real, therefore, is the diplomatic reality emerging from it. That reality has political and legal consequences. In the World Trade Organisation, for example, once countries have signed on the dotted line, the agreed texts become legally enforceable instruments. These could translate concretely into, for example, trade sanctions, at least in the armoury of those powerful countries that can apply these sanctions.

Ultimately, if the diplomatic truths are totally at variance with existential reality, then those truths are unenforceable, as could happen with the EPAs that the EU is trying hard to conclude with the ACP states. Both the North and the South negotiators in UNCTAD XII must bear this in mind when negotiating the future of this very important body in the UN system. Nonetheless, negotiated truths about reality on the ground cannot be taken lightly. They have to be taken seriously.

Why strengthening UNCTAD is also in the interest of the North

16 April 2008

It has become evident, of late, that many countries of the North, rightly or wrongly, have been perceived to want to weaken the United Nations Conference on Trade and Development (UNCTAD). Of course, this is not a uniform story. There are differences among the developed countries, just as there are among the countries of the South. It is well known, for example, that in general the Scandinavian countries favour strengthening the institutions of global multilateral governance, including the United Nations, whereas the United States, whenever possible, favours taking matters outside the United Nations system, whether they concern security, development or climate change.

Some of these differences both within and between the North and the South will, no doubt, surface at the forthcoming ministerial meeting of UNCTAD XII in Accra, Ghana, on 20–25 April 2008. There are at least 60 bracketed paragraphs in the draft negotiated text sent from Geneva. (Bracketed texts are those where there is no agreement as yet between member countries, or for which there are alternative wordings.) One of the issues so effected is whether to increase, reduce or abolish UNCTAD's intergovernmental commissions. The G77 countries want the present three commissions to be retained and a new commission added; the EU wants the three commissions to be merged into two; and some other developed countries want all commissions abolished. There are also differences on the issue of policy space. The G77 argues against the one-size-fits-all approach to macroeconomic development policy being promoted by some countries of the North and, in particular, the Bretton Woods institutions (the World Bank and the IMF), and would like instead to see UNCTAD help developing countries of the South to control their own development strategies through increased policy space. This matter was fought for and won by the South at UNCTAD XI at Sao Paulo. But the North now wants to dilute its salience in the work of UNCTAD, and is reluctant to operationalise the concept of policy space.

There are several other matters on which there are palpable differences between the North and the South. These will no doubt be thrashed out in the five days of intense negotiations that will take place at UNCTAD XII in Accra.

The objective of this editorial is not to make a case for any one or more of these contentious issues. It is, rather, to argue a more general point, namely, that if the developed countries of the North wish to weaken UNCTAD or to disempower it in critical areas of its work, then they are on the wrong track. Or, to put it more positively, it is in the interest of both the North as well as the South, to strengthen UNCTAD and not to weaken it. Why? There are several reasons, but within the limited space of this editorial, one will suffice for now.

Let us start with a recognised reality of our times, namely that the global financial system is in serious crisis. The institutions of global financial governance (the IMF and the World Bank) have neither the means nor the credibility they had in the heyday of globalisation. The North must acknowledge this. There are efforts to 'modernise' these institutions, for example, through reforming the voting formula in the IMF, but to be candid, these are palliatives. They do not address the fundamental and underlying issues that are at the bottom of the financial crisis, of which the sub-prime mortgage meltdown was only a surface phenomenon. And here, then, is the question: At which forums, within or outside the UN system, can issues of this magnitude of global significance be discussed?

Because the IMF and the World Bank have manifestly failed to address these issues, the Northern countries have chosen to discuss them in private forums such as the World Economic Forum at Davos, to which selected government representatives, the private sector and other stakeholders from the South are invited. Of late, the G7/8 countries have taken to inviting selected countries of the South to their own summits such as at Gleneagles in 2006 and in Heiligendamm in 2007. Let us face it: these summits have failed. At Gleneagles the G7 made many promises to the South, especially to African countries, for example, on the matter of aid and debt relief. The debt relief did come, but since then debts have piled up once again because the G7 at Gleneagles never even touched, let alone analysed, the fundamental and underlying causes of debt. As for aid, we are still where we have been for the last 40 years; the US and the UK are the least committed to dipping into their coffers to provide 0.7 per cent of their national incomes for development aid. At Heiligendamm, the selectively invited countries of the South were not happy at being served the dessert after the dinner had been consumed; or to put matters without flummery, they did not want to be co-opted into the pre-determined agenda of the North. At the next summit of the G7 in Tokyo there is talk of inviting up to 30 countries of the South. But that, in our view, would be an exercise in futility.

Two aspects of the changing reality must be acknowledged: one, things are falling apart; and two, there is a fundamental structural shift in economic and political power in favour of the South. It is no accident that the banks in the North are now being recapitalised by sovereign wealth from the South. This phenomenon alone is raising a number of issues of concern for the North as well as the South that need to be addressed in a proper forum that is not from the beginning dominated by the North.

The world needs a forum where there is an inclusive dialogue between *all* countries of the world, where differences and divergent viewpoints are recognised and respected, and where common ground is discovered for building workable consensus. Instead of reinventing the IMF and the World Bank with palliative reforms; instead of turning to Davos, over which governments (from the North or from the South) have no control, and which is an institution that has no operational capacity; instead of trying to co-opt selected countries from the South in the G7/8 process and creating two-tiered or three-tiered consultations that are both superficial and non-operational; why not instead strengthen the institution in the UN system that has long been mandated to be such a forum – UNCTAD? It:

- Is inclusive
- Has proven its capacity to address fundamental issues of our times and undertake serious, critical, and forward-looking analytical work
- Has had a clear development focus
- Has been a forum where consensus between nationally empowered delegations can be negotiated

- Has had and can bolster the capacity to operationalise and put into effect a consensually agreed work programme of the global community.

Why not? The UNCTAD must be provided with adequate resources by the UN system. For example, the post of deputy secretary-general has been vacant for more than a year; that and other vacancies must be filled soon. It is time the thinking public, and their representatives in government in both the North as well as the South, recognise that we are living a world that is vastly changed from the late 1940s when many of the institutions of global governance (including the Bretton Woods institutions) were created; and even from 1989 when the Berlin Wall fell and the West marched triumphantly to restructure the world to their design. It is now a different world altogether. There are past institutions that, because of the embedded power structures, are unreformable (such as the World Bank and the IMF and the Security Council of the UN), but then there are also existing multilateral institutions that can be strengthened, among them UNCTAD, and reinvented to be more in tune with the times.

Let us do this now. The UNCTAD needs to be revalidated, reinforced and revitalised for the benefit of the South and the North.

South expectations of the Development Cooperation Forum

16 March 2008

The Development Cooperation Forum (DCF) was first mentioned in the 2004 report of the secretary-general's High-level Panel on Threats, Challenges and Change. The idea was then reworked and introduced in the world summit outcome document in 2005 and further discussed in the General Assembly resolution that strengthened the UN's Economic and Social Council (ECOSOC) (A/RES/61/16). The forum was an outcome of negotiations between member states.

During the informal ministerial roundtable meeting of the ECOSOC high-level segment in 2006, an inter-active dialogue was organised around four key questions on the DCF:

- What are the major challenges affecting development cooperation?
- What innovative process could the DCF apply to foster the participation of a wide range of stakeholders?
- What would be the ideal outcome of the first DCF?
- What could be the vision for development cooperation in the year 2015?

To understand these issues from a South perspective, the South Centre undertook a desk study and interviews with some South government delegations and negotiators (mostly Geneva based), intergovernmental organisations (such as G77), intergovernmental agencies (such as FAO, IFAD, WFP), and civil society representatives. Based on this research, and on presentations made by South representatives at the high-level symposia in Vienna (April 2007) and Cairo (January 2008), the centre came up with a 'vision' of the South on DCF.

There are five major expectations that embody this vision. These are:

1. The DCF should provide an alternative to OECD–DAC on the one hand and the World Bank on the other.

2. The DCF should facilitate debate and discourse on the governance aspects of international development cooperation, which is presently asymmetrical and largely donor driven. Three kinds of asymmetries were identified: power, economic and knowledge asymmetries.

3. The DCF should link aid with broader issues of Financing for Development, and put aid into perspective (e.g. in relation to mobilisation of domestic resources, trade, investments, diaspora remittances, brain drain, and the larger systemic issues of the financial architecture). The DCF should feed into the Doha process and be proactive in influencing its outcome.

4. The DCF should encourage new donors to be more active in conversations on aid in both its normative (issues of governance, human rights and rule of law) and operational dimensions (harmonisation, accountability, division of labour and so on).

5. The DCF should facilitate or sponsor studies on exit strategies for aid-dependent countries of the South towards greater self-reliance, with target dates and indicators to assess progress. This emerged as a strong 'consensus' at the Cairo meeting.

There were several other expectations, including that the UN needs to be more adequately represented in the aid discourse and that the DCF should strengthen links between the normative and operational work of the UN on matters related to aid and development.

Ultimately, the DCF is neither a decision-making nor a negotiating body. It is a forum. That is its strength. It is an important forum for discussing all the above issues, and for encouraging a genuine dialogue between the South and the North, and also within these two broad groupings, in order to reach a common understanding of the challenges of development and the strategies to address them.

A case for radical reform of the World Trade Organisation

1 December 2008

Geneva has a surrealist atmosphere about it. It is not really part of the normal world, at least not the world of the South where two-thirds of humanity lives. The predictable public transport system timed to tick with the Swiss clock and the peaceful surroundings of Swiss mountains and Lake Geneva provide the cool ambience in which diplomats from the South and the North negotiate on matters from trade to intellectual property regimes, from disarmament to human rights. Geneva throws a comfortable veil over proceedings, making them seem aloof from the real world. The negotiations feel abstracted from the reality of power politics. The harsh and cruel realities of an often violent world out there, especially in the global South, become abstract and distant. Geneva is a synthetic, sanitised place.

This is both good and bad. It is good because it provides a certain degree of comfortable decoupling of international trade negotiations from the messy daily life of food shortages, people dying of AIDs and cholera, and terrorist attacks. But it has a reverse side to it. The existential detachment also leads to conceptual detachment. Thinking becomes universalised and idealised abstractions from reality. And when it comes to trade negotiations within the subliminal waterfront façade of the World Trade Organisation (WTO), mathematical formalism – an abstruse numbers game – takes over in an ever repeating incantation. Coefficients and percentages parody life. This is true whether the trade negotiators are working on the finer details of 'the Swiss formula' on matters related to manufacturing and industry, curiously known by a negative formulation – *Non*-Agricultural Market Access (or 'NAMA' as the experts will tell you), or 'Ag', which is the experts' lingo for agricultural negotiations.

In this rarified field of negotiations within the idiom of arithmetic, metaphors ranging from 'landing grounds' to 'taking a walk in the woods' fly from desktops, to evening party talks, to the media. Sadly, as trade negotiators take a walk in the woods, they count the trees and often lose sight of the whole forest. They may think they have won on points, scoring on the numbers game, but in the process they are often unaware that they may have managed to get lost in the forest.

The forest becomes visible, often though hindsight, at least to some honest politicians. In October 2008, for example, Bill Clinton said at the UN[1] that 'we all blew it, including me as president' by treating food crops as a commodity rather than a right of the poor. He reprimanded the World Bank, IMF and other global institutions, and cited corn subsidies and US food aid policies as key problems contributing to the global food crisis. In the WTO, however, food remains a tradable commodity, a market access issue. WTO's past follies and foibles, especially the effects of its dogged determination to push free market fundamentalism, are already visible in many parts of the world, particularly in Africa. One hopes that one day, like Clinton, the former directors general of the WTO will admit their errors. The present one, however, is pushing relentlessly along the same road.

Trade and the conditions of trade are two different things. The first is simply a word in the dictionary. The second relates to the historical and present circumstances under which countries are integrated in the global system of production and exchange. That is, trade – when taken to mean trade liberalisation, as it is in the WTO – does not automatically nor necessarily equate to improvements in the conditions under which trade takes place. Trade does not automatically equate to development. In fact, the proposition 'trade is good' is an abstract, ideological proposition, elevated as axiomatic truth in the WTO discourse. The conditions in which countries engage in trade, on the other hand, are a historically created reality that continues to the present. Why Africa, for example, should continue to remain a provider of commodities and cheap domestic and migrant labour, stems from a hard reality embedded in the global division of labour over which Africans have had little say.

These conditions are daily reinforced because the powerful countries have carrots to dangle and sticks to whip the weak so that they conform to their will. This is legitimised by the WTO and enforced by threat of sanctions. How else might you explain that African cotton farmers in their thousands are forced to surrender the right to live just because the rich and powerful US can provide subsidies to its a few hundred cotton producers? Hopefully president-elect Obama will not have to wait until retirement to acquire the Clintonite hindsight which will allow him to address this single issue.

All multilateral agencies, including the WTO, are driven by a certain balance of forces in the global domain. Asymmetrical power relations are part of the dynamics of global negotiations, whether on matters of trade or the enforcement of intellectual property rights. As for the WTO, for all intents and purposes, it has become an extension of the European agenda. The US has been in a state of semi-paralysis, in a diplomatic and moral crisis, over most of the last decade. Of all regional groupings Europe is the best organised and self-conscious political force. Of course, there is debate within Europe. Not all countries of Europe are part of the 'coalition of the willing' in alliance with the US. Nonetheless, barring countries like Norway and Switzerland that are not part of the European Union and can often voice an independent view, and notwithstanding internal differences within the union, the countries of the European Union speak with a single voice in the WTO.

The question is: How is Europe using its clout in the WTO and in the overall global trading system? It should surprise nobody if Europe uses its mind and muscle to advance European interests. To expect otherwise is to be naïve. Despite outward opulence, Europe is in serious crisis. The financial meltdown in the US has endangered the comfortable life of its bankers and citizens. Europe is even more vulnerable than the US to the risk of loss of markets and access to oil and raw materials. It must secure access to these, not only in the old empire but also in the growing markets of Brazil, China, India, Russia and South Africa. Paradoxically, these latter countries also offer the stiffest competition to Europe, especially China, in Africa. In the European media, China is often derided, for example, for its apparent lack of concern for human rights violations in Africa. However, the EU is well prepared to meet its challenges. It has a vigorous and aggressive secretariat in Brussels, driven by the Global Europe strategy, which is closely monitored and directed by Business Europe. These are its declared objectives:[2]

- Provide multilateral leadership
- Adopt an open and offensive policy on international investment

- Take decisive steps toward creating a transatlantic single market
- Deliver real market access in bilateral free trade areas (FTAs)
- Conclude an ambitious WTO Doha round
- Open new markets through bilateral trade and economic agreements.

Europe promotes its aggressive and offensive strategy with the cultured sophistication of an old empire. The EU is more skilled in the diplomacy of soft power than the US. Europe has succeeded in selling the ideology of free trade as a global public good, even to some heads of states in the South. Outside of the WTO, Europe is negotiating FTAs, and has recently harvested the CARIFORUM–EU Economic Partnership Agreement. The strange irony is that the Caribbean countries have not only surrendered much more than they would have done in the WTO (including the controversial 'Singapore issues' of investment, competition policy and government procurement, and a whole bag of other goodies) to Europe, but Europe has even managed to make the Caribbean governments (except one) feel grateful for the money it has promised to provide to buy plaster to cover their wounds. The rest of the world, especially those in the older grouping of African, Caribbean and Pacific (ACP) countries have watched in shock and incredulity. Given Europe's deftness in negotiations, backed by carrots and sticks, other ACP countries may also be lured in the same den of inequity.

In the equally dangerous den of WTO inequities, where the EU has the biggest influence, the EU will no doubt argue that the CARIFORUM countries have broken the taboo against, for example, the Singapore issues. What is good for the goose must, surely, be good for the gander. The challenge for the South, then, is how to maintain its policy space and its development agenda.

The South is, of course, not so united as Europe. The latter speaks with one voice, the South with more than a hundred. That which binds the South is their shared experience of colonialism and the sense of injustice in the trading system; that which divides them is their disparate national interests. Sometimes the South manages to sing in harmony, but when the 'big ones' among them are cajoled into the 'green room' processes of the

WTO, the harmony breaks down into a cacophony, and Europe and US are quick to take advantage of this.

Notwithstanding the cacophony, there is a song that the South can sing together, and it goes like this (in prose).

- Recognise that the South should be the agenda setters of the WTO agenda. It is where most of the global poor live. The responsibility for development cannot be handed over to those who are responsible for having created poverty and under-development in the South and their institutions.
- Recognise that development cannot be equated with neoliberal globalisation or trade liberalisation, and that the stated objective of the Doha round is development maximisation not trade liberalisation.
- Recognise that trade is secondary to production, employment and human rights. If you have no industries to produce goods, you have nothing to trade. If you do not have jobs and proper wages for the workers and peasants, you have no domestic market in which to sell goods and services. Heed the past experience of much of the South – that forced trade liberalisation has led to de-industrialisation and de-agriculturalisation especially in countries that are vulnerable to the carrots and stick policies of Europe and the US.
- Recognise the primacy of food security over trade. Do not get mesmerised by the reduction of negotiations into mathematical numbers and coefficients in the name of trade liberalisation and market access.
- Recognise the significance of the control over and ownership of natural resources – land, forest, minerals, water, minerals, fish and biogenetic resources. None of these should be sacrificial lambs on the altar of the false gods of trade.
- Recognise that intellectual property is part of humanity's heritage, acquired over centuries of painstaking research, analysis, documentation and experimentation; it a global public good; it is knowledge that cannot be monopolised by corporations for their profit maximisation; it should be a force for social good.

Finally, coming to a more controversial subject, there is a serious case to be made for a fundamental reform of the WTO, especially now that the global financial meltdown, which is worse than the 1929 crisis, has afforded an opportunity to look afresh at all institutions of global economic governance, including the WTO. It is important to understand that much of the surrealist excitement about the WTO in Geneva and in the capitals of the world is due to its two pillars. The first is that trade liberalisation has been hyped in the last 30 years as the 'engine of growth' by the Washington Consensus-dominated ideology. The second is that the negotiated texts of the WTO are binding, and so no country can ignore the WTO. The WTO is about the only organisation (besides the Security Council of the United Nations) that has teeth. The WTO can bite.

The first – *ideological* – pillar of the WTO is now fully discredited. The vacuous basis of its underlying premises has been amply exposed in the financial meltdown of the casino economy as well as by the historical experiences of the South itself. The second – *enforcement* – pillar needs to be critically reviewed. Has it really brought gains of development for the global poor? Why was the WTO given teeth in the first place, while its predecessor, the GATT, had none? It is most likely that the WTO was given teeth in the interest of Europe and the US.

While the longer-term destiny of the WTO must go on the agenda of the recent taskforce set up by the president of the General Assembly to look into the financial crisis, there is, however, one issue that the developing country members of the WTO can take on almost immediately. This is to ensure that it responds to their concerns – they after all constitute the vast majority of WTO members. The agenda-setting and process-control powers in the WTO presently lie heavily not only with the major developed members but also with the WTO secretariat. The processes of decision-making must return to the WTO members through a stronger and more influential role for the general council. The secretariat has to be in fact what they claim to be in theory: member-driven, not driving members. This is not a personal issue; it is a matter of institutional integrity.

Notes

1. As quoted by Alex Smith (2008) Associate Press, San Francisco, 26 October.
2. See www.businesseurope.eu.

A perspective on the American presidential elections

1 February 2008

The person who takes presidential authority in the United States verily affects the lives of millions of people in the world, directly or indirectly, more so than the leader of any other nation. This is because of the US's global might and reach, and the peculiarities of the American constitution that puts an incredible amount of power in the office of its president. For this reason, it is permissible to express an opinion on what kind of a leader in the US is right from a global perspective. I do this without pretending or seeking to influence the course of the present US elections.

For the American voters to prioritise the national and domestic interests of America in their choice of their president is perfectly understandable. Nonetheless, an enlightened voter would define 'national interest' broadly enough to include a global perspective. Unfortunately, that perspective, because of the record of the US during the last decade, can best be described in largely negative terms. It is a perspective that jeopardises the lives and wellbeing of ordinary people in the rest of the world, the safety and sustainability of the natural environment – a milieu that knows no electoral boundaries – and the stability of the global financial system.

It follows that the president of the United States must have a vision that goes beyond a narrowly conceived national interest; it must be a national vision that embodies the global imperatives. In their presidential campaigns, US presidential candidates must also aim to educate and enlighten the voters, help them understand their wider responsibilities beyond America. It is this kind of enlightened vision that was so appealing about President John F. Kennedy. It is true to say that he had 'electoral support' beyond the borders of the United States.

It is from such a perspective and from that of the two-thirds of humanity that live in the global South that we identify certain concerns which an aspiring presidential candidate must attempt seriously to address. They include the following:

1. Openness to sharing global knowledge. The monopolisation and commercialisation of knowledge by private corporations for profit is the most critical obstacle to the development of the South. Private appropriation of public knowledge is indefensible under any political system that seeks moral legitimacy, as any global power must. Allowing corporations to 'own' biological diversity and the traditional knowledge of the South and of indigenous peoples without fair and justified returns to them is indefensible.

2. At the core of the poverty of the poor in the global South lies a system of global production and exchange that, for the last 30 years, has been marketed and globalised under the so-called Washington consensus, which, so far, none of the Presidential candidates has dared to challenge. Why not? They must do so, even if this means a radical paradigmatic shift in their own thinking.

3. That system of production and consumption has allowed the citizens of the United States to consume six per cent more than they produce, which translates into trillions of dollars that pour into the US every year, mainly from the global South. This is unfair. What is worse is that such an unfair distribution of the world's resources is sustained by credit expansion and a financial and banking system that in recent months has erupted into the sub-prime mortgage crisis in the US, which has now jeopardised the financial stability of the rest of the world. Corrective measures need to be taken both at the national and global levels, for which proper consultative mechanisms have to be established with the political leaders of the global South, as well as of Europe, Russia and Japan.

4. It must be explained to the voters in the United States that a monopolar world has now given way to a multipolar world. There is not one centre but several: countries like Brazil, China, the Gulf states, India and Russia wield considerable control over global resources and their use and distribution. These new realities must direct a new US president to throw his or her authority to reconfigure the architecture of the major institutions of global governance, such as the United Nations system, the World Bank, the IMF and the WTO. These new realities, too, have not featured significantly enough in the election campaigns of most of the presidential candidates.

5. The environment and climate change have become political bywords in recent times. And yet, their development component is mostly excluded from public discourse. For example, the widely acclaimed documentary *An Inconvenient Truth* is uncomfortably silent about the developmental dimension. The UN's Intergovernmental Panel on Climate Change (IPCC) predicts that climate change will have a graver effect on Africa than on any other continent. Of the 800 million people living in the dryland areas, it is estimated that up to 250 million will face water shortages by 2020. The new leadership of the United States must face up to its responsibility towards Africa beyond its present preoccupation with security and terrorist threats.

6. American philanthropy is a good virtue. Ironically, philanthropy thrives with increasing social fragmentation between classes, gender, races and nations. The greater the rich–poor gap, the more wealth there is in the hands of a few for philanthropy. But the need for philanthropy should not arise if wealth is shared fairly and equitably in the first place. This is true at the global level just as it is at the national. The world's poor must not be at the mercy of charity. They must have the dignity of decent work and choices that make life meaningful.

The role of civil society in national space

16 August 2008

For 30 years (from the mid 1970s to the end of the last century) many governments in the South, especially in the low and middle-income countries, surrendered their right to make macroeconomic policies to the Bretton Woods institutions (BWIs) – the International Monetary Fund (IMF) and the World Bank. The BWIs' so-called Structural Adjustment Programmes (SAPs) advocated, among other things, free market liberalisation, fiscal austerity, privatisation and marketisation of essential social services such as health, education and water. The most potent tool for enforcing SAPs was so-called 'development aid', or official development assistance (ODA). Looking back it is truly amazing that even tiny amounts of ODA with BWI conditionalities were able to tie up the entire national revenues of these countries and shape their 'development' strategies. This is because the politicians and bureaucracies of these countries had internalised the Washington Consensus, the ideological bedrock of these policies. For this reason, none of these governments ever pointed out that the so-called consensus was never negotiated in any intergovernmental process, either in the United Nations, or even within the BWIs.

However, these policies were fundamentally flawed, as the wisdom of hindsight has shown. As argued by the BWIs, these policies were presumed, among other things, to weed out inefficient industries in the South and make those left behind more competitive in a globalising world. They led, instead, to rapid deindustrialisation of most of these countries, especially in Africa and Latin America.

The civil society organisations (CSOs) in these countries were the first to raise the alarm. The effects of SAPs were disastrous, especially for poorer people. In the 1990s protests against the IMF-induced policies became widespread, and food riots spread from one country to another. The CSOs launched a global campaign against the BWIs under the clarion call '50 years are enough'.

That, however, did not end the domination of the BWIs, who decided that it was time to involve civil society. The BWIs initiated the PRSPs (Poverty Reduction Strategy Papers) and for a while successfully marketed these as a 'step in the right direction', suggesting they were passing 'ownership' of the SAPs to the countries themselves and involving CSOs, the presumptive representatives of the grassroots. With generous funds from Northern donors a large number of Southern CSOs were co-opted into what looked on the surface like people's involvement in PRSPs, but what in fact was a predetermined agenda driven by the donors and BWIs.

Almost another decade went by, and the PRSPs also failed, their cover of 'recipient country ownership' blown by the continuing failure to lift the masses in the 'rising tide of globalisation'. Poverty remained stubborn, despite the IMF and World Bank's anodyne figures that pretended that things were better. Unable to provide better strategies, the donors and the BWIs shifted the blame for enduring poverty to Southern governments. The macroeconomic policies, they argued, were not flawed; the problem lay with poor governance, corruption, and a lack of Southern government accountability to their populations. Between 1991 and 2004, the BWIs and donors shifted their aid conditionalities from purely macroeconomic policies to governance. According to figures computed from World Bank data, the financial and private sector development conditionalities levelled out, but the conditionalities associated with the public sector, governance and the rule of law steadily increased from 10 per cent in 1996 to 45 per cent in 2004.[1] According to UNCTAD, during 2003–05, the rich countries committed $1.3 billion of ODA funds to improving governance in the LDCs, and only $12 million to agricultural improvement.

It is also about this time that the language of 'aid effectiveness' emerged in the vocabulary of the donors and the BWIs. The Paris Declaration on Aid Effectiveness (PDAE) of the Organisation of Economic Cooperation and Development (OECD) emerged from this background. In a closely argued analysis, *Ending Aid Dependence* shows that the underlying basic philosophy of PDAE is that for aid to be 'effective', the governance of the recipient countries needs to be improved and be accountable to the donors and domestic CSOs. PDAE argues skillfully, using laudable principles such as ownership, mutual accountability and aid predictability. *As with the Washington Consensus, however, the PDAE pretends to be a 'consensus', but it was never negotiated through any regular intergovernmental process.*

Note

1. See Y. Tandon (2008) *Ending Aid Dependence*, Geneva and Oxford, South Centre and Fahamu.

Part II
Some specific issues

3

Industrialisation, technology, innovation and intellectual property

Introduction

For the last three decades we have lived in a topsy-turvy world where trade is privileged over industry and finance over production. For sure, trade and finance are important, but both are only means to encourage production and industry and not the other way around. Now both the trading and the financing worlds are in deep crises, and old-time neoliberal ideologists are grudgingly talking about how to restore the 'the real economy' having subordinated it to the demands of free trade and financial liberalisation. The editorial 'Putting production over trade and finance' addresses some of these issues.

When it comes to production, the key is industrialisation, including the application of technological knowledge to agriculture. Agriculture and industry are in many ways distinct operations, but their integration is the basis of development. In the developed countries of the North the two are integrated; they have industrialised agriculture. In the developing countries there is a huge gap between mechanised, commercialised agriculture on the one hand and subsistence farming that employs hoes for ploughing and animals for traction. It is imperative that the South develops and harnesses its innovative capacity to build its knowledge industry. The monopolisation of knowledge in the name of 'intellectual property' is one of the biggest obstacles to development and the dissemination of technology. This is the theme of the essay on 'Rising to the challenge of innovation'.

How the developed countries of the North monopolise knowledge and use intellectual property (IP) to control production and trade is the theme of the next essay on 'WIPO, WCO, intellectual property and border guards'. IP enforcement is a contentious terrain. The developed countries have been pushing one-sidedly for the enforcement of IP right holders, while the developing countries have been demanding that IP rights be balanced against the right to development. The South Centre, its member states, and sympathetic non-governmental organisations (NGOs) have managed to block the attempts of the North to use the World Customs Organisation (WCO) to enforce a Standards Employed by Customs for Uniform Rights Enforcement (SECURE), and thus enhanced the possibility for the developing countries to innovate their own technologies, for example, for their manufacturing, agriculture, communication and the pharmaceutical industries.

Putting production over trade and finance

1 February 2009

One of the most logically flawed elements of the neoliberal globalisation paradigm of the last three decades has been the privileging of trade over industry and finance over production. Symptomatically, the Geneva-based World Trade Organisation (WTO) has been on the global agenda and under the media spotlight more than the United Nations Industry and Development Organisation (UNIDO). It should have been the other way round. Industry precedes trade; if there is no production there is no trade. One of the more hopeful side effects of the present crumbling of the Doha round of trade negotiations is that people will begin to prioritise production and industrialisation over trade. Certainly, a development friendly outcome of the Doha round would have been a good thing, but the fact that it is at stalemate is indicative of a deeper malaise in the system. That it should happen at the same time as the collapse of the global financial system is no accident. The simultaneous near-death, or at least illlegitimisation, of both the WTO and the Bretton Woods institutions (the World Bank and the International Monetary Fund) is related to a dual weakness in the global economic system – the dominance of trade over industry and of finance over production.

Of the two, the latter is a more serious problem. Financialisation of production has put a premium on speculative profits, often made out of fictitious money or credit, rather than where the emphasis should be – on production itself. Ponzi schemes (fraudulent investment operations that pay returns to investors out of the money paid by subsequent investors rather than from profit) of the kind run by the $50 billion collapsed empire of Bernard Madoff duped millions into believing that they were putting their investments into the real economy, whereas they were only putting these into a deep black hole. Even reputable banks, mostly in the Western world, were fooled. As for trade, the prevailing neoliberal dogma that places it above industry is the second Achilles' heel of the global system and is indeed linked to the first one. In fact, trading in money (money markets, Ponzi schemes, currency, arbitage, hedge futures trading, financial intermediation) constitutes almost 98 per cent of all financial transactions; only 2 per cent or less actually finance trade in real goods. This is the topsy-turvy world in which we live. Achilles the ancient Greek hero of the Trojan War had only one heel that was vulnerable, but the present global system's two heels (trade and finance) have serious defects that render the system exposed to manipulations by crooks and cranks.

This is not to underestimate the importance of either finance or trade. What is produced must be financed and traded. Finance is a means to production, but only one of at least three other ingredients – labour power, natural resources and entrepreneurial skills. In the present global system of production, banks and entrepreneurs are inordinately privileged over labour and natural resources (a CEO of a big multinational can earn a salary of over a million dollars a month whereas a worker gets a tiny fraction of this, especially if he or she – especially, she – is located in the countries of the South). That fundamentally explains why rich countries become richer and poor countries stay poor.

Trade is important too. After goods are produced they must be consumed. Of course, not all that is produced is necessarily traded; subsistence farmers in much of the South, for example, consume what they produce without going through the market. Nonetheless, markets are important for the distribution of goods produced, and for realising the value contained in the goods so that the production cycle begins again. However, the present global trading system is heavily loaded against the countries of the South for both historical and structural reasons. The natural resources of the South are seriously undervalued in the global market. If you factor in the real value of the labour power of the workers of the South, and add the environmental cost of exploitation of the South's resources, then the countries in the South should be getting at least four or five times more value than they currently receive. This is the second fundamental reason why rich countries further enrich themselves at the cost of the poor countries.

Even when it comes to production, there is an anomaly in the present system of production. Besides the undervaluation of labour power and the natural resources of the South, the combination of factors of production is heavily weighted in favour of the suppliers of capital and patented technology. And there is very little of what is called 'the transfer of technology'. A study carried out by UNCTAD in 2007 on the least developed countries (LDCs) found that most LDCs have opened up their economies to global trade and are highly integrated in the global economy, but they are not climbing the economic and technological ladder. The study covered 11 LDCs over a two-year period (2004–06) including six African and four Asian countries and Haiti. Based on this, the report showed that the LDCs continue to import high-value machinery and equipment, which are paid for out of low-value exports in the production chain and a long-term decline in the terms of trade. Domestic firms and farms in LDCs have low technology capabilities. Out of the 24 value chains of LDC exports, upgrading has occurred in only nine since the 1990s, and downgrading in 12 representing 52 per cent of LDC exports. The study of 155 firms in Bangladesh, for example, showed that there was no development of technological capacity in agro-processing, textiles, garments and pharmaceuticals. As for the much-touted myth that foreign direct investments (FDIs) are a means of transferring technological know-how, the study found that the FDIs have not helped LDCs much. The problem is not a lack of opening up to foreign investors but, rather, it is the quality of integration of transnational corporations (TNCs) into host countries' economies. Most FDIs concentrated on mineral extraction in enclaves with little spillover into the domestic economy.

The UNCTAD study put this all down to 'economic liberalisation without learning'; global integration without innovation. This resulted in the increasing marginalisation of 767 million people in the LDCs. The LDCs are locked into low value-added commodity production and low-skill manufacturing. This is in sharp contrast to the East Asian countries such as Japan, Korea and Taiwan that encouraged technological learning during their early phase of industrialisation.

There are at least two lessons to draw from history and the current phase of capitalist globalisation. One is that the developing countries must have policy space in order to design their economic roadmap. This is what is seriously compromised in the dogmatic pursuit of globalisation. Market fundamentalism has replaced common sense. The second is to underscore the centrality of knowledge, technological learning and innovation for development. Knowledge is the key to global production and competition. The trend of economic globalisation is increasingly towards the development of intellectual rather than physical assets. It is here that most developing countries (and not only the LDCs) are still hostage to the monopolisation of knowledge. The knowledge divide between the rich and poor nations has increased, especially over the last three decades of capitalist globalisation. The current intellectual property (IP) regimes lock patented technologies away from the reach of the developing economies. Indeed, intellectual property is the last refuge of the industrialised countries.

Within the WTO framework, the Trade Related Investment Measures (TRIMS) discourage local content requirements thus killing effective industrial policy and learning, which is the basis for industrialisation. The Trade Related Intellectual Property Rights (TRIPS) involve very high transaction costs in complex procedural requirements in implantation and enforcement that the poorest countries of the South cannot afford. Furthermore, the developed countries drive hard bargains against the poor countries in the free trade agreements (FTAs) with them. For example, Article 11D of the IP agreement between the US and Cambodia in 1996 limits Cambodia's flexibility for a unique system for plant protection. In the economic partnership agreements (EPAs) between the European Union and the African, Caribbean and Pacific (ACP) countries the EU has sought to include patenting for biotechnology inventions and plant varieties and legal protection of databases as part of IP rights, which go far beyond the requirements of WTO compatibility.

And that is not to mention the highly controversial debate on technology transfer with regard to climate change. It is well recognised that the world has to move towards a low carbon economy, but how to do this is a challenge. A lot of the success depends on the transfer of technology for emission reduction and adaptation from the North to the South. The North would want to define this as part of ODA or aid, but it should not be. It is part of the commitment that the rich countries have made to the poor countries in the United Nations Framework Convention on Climate Change (UNFCCC). The bigger problem, however, is not money or even the technology. The bigger problem is the IP content of the technology because, through it, the corporations of the North that have the technologies can use the IP regimes to control the technological processes necessary for emission control and adaptation.

At the heart of the technology is innovation, and at the heart of innovation is the economics of knowledge production and dissemination. The Northern governments, aided and abetted by their corporations, have created a formidable array of national and international structures such as the Anti-Counterfeit Trade Agreement (ACTA), the Global IP Centre (GIPC), the International Medicinal Products Anti-Counterfeit Taskforce (IMPACT), and the Standards Employed by Customs for Uniform Rights Enforcement (SECURE). In order to secure legitimacy and enforcement instrumentalities, the North has smuggled some of them into the body fabric of intergovernmental organisations, for example, SECURE within the World Customs Organisation (WCO) and IMPACT within the World Health Organisation (WHO). The resultant multi-headed monster then created breathes more fire and generates more heat than the mythical Chinese dragon.

Putting production above trade and finance is an imperative for development. But the road is paved with deep potholes and along the way there are fire-breathing monsters. Who said development is a linear, struggle-free process?

Rising to the challenge of innovation

16 October 2007

The link between innovation and patents is often misunderstood or deliberated misrepresented. One does not necessarily measure the other. Patents may encourage innovation but they could equally discourage it. The usual argument is that patents are necessary for investors to put money into risky ventures. However, studies show that a strong patent system does not lead to innovation but to monopolisation of knowledge through, for example, cross-licensing agreements between transnational corporations and the creation of litigation-free zones. Also, governments subsidise national champions for research and development and undermine competition.

Evidence also shows that the patent system acts differently depending on the industry and on the market. The report of the Commission on Intellectual Property Rights, Public Health and Innovation (CIPIH) that was established under the World Health Organisation (WHO) showed that where the market has little purchasing power patents may not stimulate research and development, or bring new products to market. A case in point is the patent system in the pharmaceutical industry. Here the patent system may cause a significant increase in the price of medicines needed for diseases that affect millions of poor people in developing countries, depriving them of access to necessary medicines.

The developing countries are not necessarily opposed to the patent system. They too want to benefit from knowledge resources. Protecting local innovation must remain a key priority for them. Strong and fair patent laws may be a mechanism to do so. However, developing countries are opposed to monopolisation of knowledge and the structural and historical inequities embedded in the present patent regime. It is a serious hindrance to development and to innovation. This is especially the case when these inequities are embedded in sanctions-bearing treaties such as the one on Trade-Related Intellectual Property Rights (TRIPs) in the WTO. The TRIPS Agreement has some flexibilities that allow room for the South to develop its patent laws according to its needs and priorities. But prevailing monopoly interests, backed by some powerful countries, inhibit the ability of the developing countries to use those flexibilities.

Currently, WHO members are discussing in the Intergovernmental Working Group on Innovation, Public Health and Intellectual Property Rights how to design a global strategy and plan of action to drive research and innovation on diseases that disproportionately affect developing countries. There is clear recognition from both the North and South that the patent system has not been able to respond to these needs and that global cooperation is required to address the gaps.

The South must harness its innovative capacity. This requires building appropriate and, where necessary, alternative models to those of the North. This does not mean backtracking on their international obligations. The South now has new opportunities to rise to the challenge of innovation. It must bring upfront its own proactive development agendas in forums such as the WTO and WIPO.

There is already some progress in this direction. For example, the Development Agenda, a South initiative for change in the international intellectual property system, was finally adopted, after a long struggle, by all member states at the World Intellectual Property Organisation (WIPO) general assembly in September 2007. Another example is the International Symposium on 'Examining Intellectual Property Enforcement from a Development Perspective' recently hosted by the South Centre.

These developments in WIPO, in the WTO and in institutions such as the South Centre (and the centre is only one among many centres of excellence in the South) are reflections of history in the making for a framework alternative agenda on intellectual property that is pro-development and pro-poor.

WIPO, WCO, intellectual property and border guards

16 May 2008

Intellectual property (IP) enforcement is a contentious terrain. The developed countries have been pushing one-sidedly for the enforcement of IP right holders, while the developing countries have been demanding that IP rights be balanced against the right to development. Against this background, the attempt to get the World Customs Organisation (WCO) to adopt the Provisional Standards Employed by Customs for Uniform Rights Enforcement (SECURE) at its council meeting in June 2008 poses a serious challenge to the developing countries. If adopted in its current form, these standards would seriously compromise both the WIPO development agenda and the Trade-Related Intellectual Property Rights (TRIPS) flexibilities. The policy space that the developing countries need in order to access knowledge and technology for their industrialisation would diminish.

In October 2007, the World Intellectual Property Organisation (WIPO), after long and arduous negotiations between the developed and developing countries, finally adopted the Development Agenda. The objective of the agenda is to promote technological innovation as well as the transfer and dissemination of technology to promote the social and economic welfare of developing countries and in such a manner as to balance the rights and obligations of the producers and users of technology.

Now that the developing countries have succeeded in getting the Development Agenda into the WIPO, the developed countries have moved to the less well-known World Customs Organisation (WCO), an intergovernmental organisation that operates through customs administrations which (so far) have a limited mandate. The SECURE Working Group is dominated by a few developed countries and a core group of Northern corporate rightholders (NCRs). The NCRs participate on an equal footing with governments. Participation by developing countries, on the other hand, is bureaucratic (mostly officials from customs administrations), and not adequately (indeed, not at all) guided by their political bosses.

The objective of SECURE is to enlarge the powers of customs administrations and 'border guards' to do the work for the NCRs as the watchdogs of IP enforcement, and to give them authority well beyond their current mandate. The standards included in the provisional SECURE on 'IPR Legislative and Enforcement Regime Development' represent a significant departure from the existing standards of the TRIPS Agreement. This represents yet another attempt by developed countries to promote through the backdoor a 'TRIPS-Plus-Plus' agenda on international border enforcement. Although the SECURE standards are described by the WCO as 'voluntary', in future these are likely to evolve into mandatory standards, as happened with the model provisions of the Framework of Standards to Secure and Facilitate Global Trade (SAFE) adopted in 1995 and revised in 2001 and 2004.

Given its serious TRIPS-Plus-Plus nature, it is time for developing countries to coordinate their positions and get their political act together before the June session of the council. They should make all-out efforts to prevent the adoption of the proposed SECURE by the WCO council session in June 2008.

There are a number of complex issues on IP enforcement that ought to be properly studied first, and the present content of SECURE needs to be considerably modified before it can be given the green light. The South Centre has taken some initiatives in this regard. For example, in February 2008, the South Centre held a side event on the occasion of the Global Congress on Counterfeiting and Piracy in Dubai. At this event a number of customs officials from the developing countries were, for the first time, exposed to an alternative to the dominant WCO-NCR perspective, especially on the very complex and technical subject of IP enforcement. The South and the South Centre do support the harmonisation of IP enforcement rules, but this should be done in harmony with the development agenda now adopted by the WIPO and in conformity with the flexibilities provided in the TRIPs of the WTO. For example, according to TRIPs, border measures apply only to importation of counterfeit trademarks or pirated copyright goods. There is a significant distinction between IPRs violations and product falsification (e.g. in pharmaceuticals). SECURE applies border measures for IPR violations, and this goes far beyond the provisions of TRIPs. Furthermore, there are economic and legal aspects of enforcement costs that are often not fully understood, let alone incorporated, in the calculations of customs administrations in the countries of the South.

The Development Agenda in the WIPO is about moving beyond a narrow NCR-centric perspective of intellectual property. The WCO, too, should embrace a development perspective instead of putting the narrowly conceived protection of rights at the centre of everything. IPRs are a means and not an end. They are a means to equitable development of societies that have been deprived, ever since the colonisation of the South, of access to knowledge and the infrastructure of promoting innovation in their own countries. The WCO must therefore include the perspectives of a broader constituency of non-IP holders in both the developed and developing countries, especially now that issues such as climate change and food insecurity are looming large in global discourse. For example, the strong intellectual property protection of genetically modified organisms (GMOs) has affected public research and farmers' rights to seeds, as pointed out by the International Assessment of Agricultural Knowledge, Science and Technology for Development (IAASTD). The report of the IAASTD, a work of 400 scientific experts, criticised the present trade and IP regimes as favouring the rich and the rich countries to the detriment of the poor.

As we go to press, we learn that Francis Gurry has been elected as the new director-general of the WIPO. He will take office in September when he will be officially confirmed by the general assembly of the WIPO. In congratulating Mr Gurry on his election to this very important position, we wish to encourage him to try and develop a positive coalition of forces (non-governmental as well as governmental) that will change the present NCR-dominated culture of the WIPO to one that is more balanced. In this balancing exercise, and to the extent that his mandate will allow him, the mainstreaming of development agenda concepts into the WIPO institutional framework and programmatic work would be a critical responsibility of his office. He will find in the IAASTD report nuggets of gold that he can bring to the WIPO, which sorely and surely needs a culture overhaul. He will also find in the South Centre a useful ally.

4

Climate, energy and the food challenge

Introduction

The world is caught up in a fossil-fuel trap. For centuries, solar power was the source of all energy. Indeed, all older civilisations worshipped the Sun in one form or another. With the industrial revolution came the revolutionary shift from the open solar system to the closed energy system, based on fossil fuels, which is at the root of global warming. Fossil fuels are also a depleting resource. The immediate challenge of our times is two-fold: a) how to manage fossil-fuel based industrialisation so that all human beings have a fair and equitable share of energy and the prospect of development; and b) how to radically change our lifestyles in order to become less dependent on fossil fuels whose global warming potential endangers the life of the only planet we know. In the long run, it is necessary, once again, to worship the Sun, and return to the open solar-powered energy systems. This is the theme of 'Open versus closed energy systems and climate change'.

Against the background of the imperatives of the immediate, the next essay, 'Bali must put development squarely on the climate change regime', written on the eve of the Bali conference on climate change, argues that climate change requires of the global community a much greater level of coordination, coherence, and unity of thought and action than it has hitherto shown. This requires a comprehensive and integrated policy framework as the basis for global action. This must reflect both the concerns of developing countries for a sustained and sustainable development and the global concern to substantially reduce greenhouse gas emissions and mitigate and adapt to global warming. The principle of common but differentiated responsibility and respective capabilities, agreed at Rio, remains the essential basis of negotiating a fair deal between the industrialised and the developing countries.

If the above course is not followed, then the biggest burden will fall on the poorer nations, and within them, on the poorest people. Global food prices have been rising steadily since 2002. Global hot spots of unrest caused by spiralling food prices include Burkina Faso, Cameroon, Egypt, Haiti, Indonesia, Ivory Coast, Mauritania, Mozambique and Senegal. Among the most popular suggested causes of the food crisis are: global warming that has disrupted the balance of the natural systems of air, water and weather patterns essential for food production; the rising fuel prices pushing up cost of fertilisers, transport, etc; and the conversion of food land to biofuels. This and other related issues are discussed in the editorial 'Why is a proper analysis of the current food crisis so important?'

Sadly, neoliberal economists see in the food crisis not the human dimension, but an opportunity for investors to make a profit. At a workshop organised by the South Centre in June 2008, one expert from the UN's Food and Agriculture Organisation (FAO) said that high food prices provide an opportunity for capital to return to profitable investment in agriculture. What we may be witnessing soon, he said, is a 'renaissance' for the agricultural sector. His is by no means a solitary voice. The votaries of 'green revolution' have been sermonising on this theme for decades. But in a world of food production and distribution where just ten corporations control 57 per cent of the total sales of the world's leading 30 retailers and account for 37 per cent of the revenues earned by the world's top 100 food and beverage companies, the 'green revolution' is likely to augment the profits of these corporations rather than solve the problem of hunger. This is the theme of the essay 'Global food crisis: alternatives to the green revolution'.

Open versus closed energy systems and climate change

16 February 2009

The immediate priority for all concerned about climate change, to be sure, is to find the ways and means to achieve the objective set by the United Nations Framework Convention on Climate Change (UNFCCC) and Kyoto and Bali as we move towards Copenhagen. These must be done on the basis of the following principles:

- The recognition of climate as a global public good
- Equity and common but differentiated responsibilities and respective capabilities for climate change
- Factoring into any negotiations the historical responsibility of the industrialised countries for global warming
- The primacy of the United Nations process
- The commitment to broader human rights and development goals.

Equity demands that in the long run the world moves towards equal per capita emissions at ecologically sustainable levels. Realism demands that we all must change our lifestyles. If everybody were to emulate the Northern lifestyle then we will need many more planets, but we only have this one with its finite resources. We are already reaching critical tipping points in large parts of the world such as in the Arctic sea, the Atlantic deep water formation, the meltdown of the Greenland ice sheet, permafrost and tundra loss, etc. Small island states, such as the Maldives and Tuvalu, are already facing the almost certainty of a catastrophe in the not too distant a future that could cause their countries to drown from rising sea levels.

The challenge humanity faces is to balance the demands and needs of the immediate in the ongoing negotiations on climate change under the UNFCCC with a move (also starting immediately) towards the longer-term objective of a sensible approach to lifestyle and the search for alternative sources of renewable energy and replenishing of life-sustaining resources. The mitigation measures that are in place or in the pipeline for transport, building construction, industry, agriculture, urban planning, etc, are all very well, but unless an alternative source of energy is found – and quickly – all these mitigation measures will not ensure climate security while meeting the fair demand for equitable development for all the citizens of the world. A changing lifestyle is the most pressing immediate to long-term objective.

The other immediate to long-term pressing need is the search for a viable alternative source of energy to either hydrocarbons or nuclear. The Ecuadorian Yasuni project of leaving oil in the ground is an excellent initiative. The international community should seriously consider paying half the cost to the people of Ecuador for not bringing oil to the surface. If a small step, at least it is a step in the right direction, given that self-indulgent oil consumption is one of the major causes of global warming.

The bigger challenge is to reverse the 300-year-old dependence on fossil fuels since the beginning of the industrial revolution. The reasons are not hard to find:

- Fossil fuel is a finite resource, no matter how hard profit-driven corporations try to persuade us that there is enough potential coal, oil and gas buried in land and under the seas.
- Even if 2000 levels of emissions are reduced by half by 2050, they would be around 450 parts per million of carbon dioxide, which would still mean a rise of 2–2.4°C in temperature by 2050; whether this will stabilise the climate is still debatable.
- The global energy crisis and the rush for biofuels have serious implications for food security across the world, especially in the poor South.
- Above all, and this is often overlooked in climate change debates, the scramble for oil and gas is a major source of conflict in the world (Caucasus, Middle East, Africa, Latin America). It has led, and could continue to lead, to increased instances of war, violence and violations of human rights.

Where do we begin and what do we do? There are, of course, many ideas that are currently being debated on the issue of climate change. This has been going on for at least the last four decades since the publication of Rachel Carlson's *Silent Spring* in 1962, widely credited with motivating the environmental movement. We have moved some distance, no doubt, but not far enough. The difficulty of mobilising the necessary political will among the developed countries of the world and finding the needed financial and technological resources are major challenges. There is, however, one idea that has not received as much scientific attention or multi-country cooperation, or even discussion, as it deserves. This is the question of *how gradually to shift out of the fossil-fuel based closed energy system to a solar power-based open system*. We write as laymen in the hope of encouraging a more serious debate on the subject.

While solar energy is recognised as an important source of energy, it is treated largely from an economic perspective and even more narrowly from the profit-seeking perspective of global corporations. This disadvantages solar power against fossil fuel. Innovation and technology development in the area of harnessing solar energy is excruciatingly slow and expensive. Presently, Japan, Germany and China appear to be at the forefront of research and technology development in the field of harnessing solar power. Japan accounts for nearly 50 per cent of the total solar cell production in the world and exports about 30 per cent of its production. Although Germany is not an ideal location for solar energy it has become the largest solar thermal market in Europe. The German Federal Association of the Solar Industry reported that there were 1,300,000 solar plants in Germany in 2006. China too is making efforts to harness solar power. By 2010 it hopes to generate about 300 megawatts of solar energy (presently less than 10 megawatts), but this is still a tiny fraction of the country's total electricity production of approximately 300,000 megawatts. All these efforts are commendable but they are woefully puny compared to what is needed. Odd as it may sound, and despite all the hoo-hah about global warming, the world has not sufficiently woken up to the dangers of the closed fossil-based system, and to the absolute imperative of shifting to an open solar-based system. It is necessary to raise the level of the debate to the higher level of philosophy and culture as well as science and economics in order to give it a necessary boost.

One of the accidents of history is that the industrial revolution began in England where the source of energy was totally revolutionised from the previous, largely open, system of solar energy to the closed system of fossil-fuel energy. Had some of the older civilisations survived, the sources of energy to fuel the industrial revolution might have been very different. Instead of exploiting fossil fuels they might have developed technology relevant to the sun as the source of all energy. This is, of course, speculative, but it is not too far-fetched. The Sun was worshipped in most ancient civilisations. In ancient Egypt, the chief cult centre of Ra was based in Heliopolis (ancient Inunu) meaning 'City of the Sun'. In ancient China, sun worship was a daily ritual, and according to paleographers, the words Bin Ri, Chu Ri and Ru Ri were all sacrificial rites to the Sun. In Ancient India the Sun (Surya) was worshipped as the Sun-god since the Vedic times. In ancient Greece the sun was personified as Helius and, together with Selene (the moon) and Eos (the dawn), Greek life was connected with the celestial. The ancient Maya were good astronomers and life revolved around the celestial movements of the sun, moon and planets. Even in the more recent Pre-Columbian Meso-America, in the Aztec civilisation for example, the days, months, and cosmic cycles all revolved around the Sun calendar. All these civilisations declined one by one, or were defeated, as history tells us, by 'barbarian' cultures. By the time we come to the industrial revolution in Europe, Sun worship had declined and the source of energy had shifted dramatically to fossil fuels. These days sun worshippers are to be found only on 'sun and sand' beaches.

The world has shifted radically to the fossil-fuel based *closed system of energy*. Both fossil fuel and nuclear are parts of the 'closed energy system'. In the closed system there is no escape from global warming. Fossil-fuel emissions are trapped in the atmosphere, and nuclear waste has to be buried deep in the ground for millions of years. All the post-industrial technological innovation is based on the closed system – from transport to house construction, to industrial and agricultural development. Emissions are trapped in the closed system. In the sun-powered *open energy system*, on the other hand, there is a free flow of cosmic energy that lights, heats and burns, creating an open cycle of the energy used, dissipated and returned.

This is not to argue that we go back to sun worship, like our ancients. That, by the way, may not be such a bad idea after all;

at least sun worship could re-energise a new (old) global secular culture, and in the (rather unlikely) prospect of it replacing the present religious diversity and chaos, it might enhance the prospects of a more peaceful world. This, however, is a side argument. The main point here is to argue that we go back to the open energy system powered by the sun rather than the one powered by fossil fuels or nuclear energy. It is necessary to take the debate beyond the narrow calculations of profit and economics. It is a much bigger debate. Of course, economics cannot be left out, but if in a matter of a few months the industrialised countries of the North can mobilise billions of dollars to save the banking system from total collapse, how much more can the world as a whole raise to save our endangered planet from burning out?

If nothing else, the United Nations could put on its agenda a discussion of how the world might return to the open energy solar system; it could, for example, establish a group of eminent scientists, palaeontologists, philosophers, environmentalists and economists to study the subject and report to it. Some high-level research institutions of major countries could collaborate to create a new international body that could undertake further research into the solar system; such an institution could be named, for example, RaRiHe (the 'Ra' of Egypt, 'Ri' of China and 'He' from the Greek Helius). This is not being supercilious, melodramatic or hyperbolic. The scale of the challenge and the responsibility of the present generation to future ones is a serious matter. What the world is doing through the painstaking process of negotiations on climate change is too superficial, too little, and dangerously too slow.

Bali must put development squarely on the climate change regime

1 December 2007

Our civilisation has entered a new and critical stage. Scientific evidence fully supports the conclusion that climate change is largely human-induced and will affect us all. But the causes and the impacts of climate change do not relate to all of us in equal measures. The industrialised countries bear greater historical responsibility for causing it while the developing countries bear the greater adverse impact. Developing countries have ended up paying the price for energy profligacy that occurred as select countries became industrialised.

The Intergovernmental Panel on Climate Change (IPCC) projects that unless current rates of greenhouse gas (GHG) emissions are drastically cut and reversed, global average temperatures will rise by at least 2°C by 2050. Much before that, the expected 1°C rise by 2020 will have a devastating impact on the developing countries. The developing countries could get locked into a condition where millions of their people remain poor and marginalised. The least developed countries (LDCs) may forever end up losing the possibility of providing people with better lives, and some small island states may even have their territorial survival jeopardised. The enormity of this challenge is not fully grasped by stakeholders.

Addressing climate change requires of the global community a much greater level of coordination, coherence, and unity of thought and action than it has hitherto shown. A comprehensive and integrated policy framework is called for to form the basis for global action. This must genuinely reflect the needs of developing countries for sustained development to remove millions from the poverty bracket and the global concerns to substantially reduce GHG emissions and adapt to global warming. The principle of common but differentiated responsibility and respective capabilities agreed at Rio remains the fundamental basis for negotiating a fair deal between the industrialised and developing countries.

The fulfilment of the right to development in an equitable and sustainable manner must be linked to the establishment of a supportive international economic system to stabilise climate change. A fairer and more equitable global arrangement needs to be created in which developing countries are able to increase energy use commensurate to their path to sustainable development. The costs of mitigation and adaptation must be based on equitable burden sharing, taking into account the historical responsibilities and also the energy needs of those whose development was hitherto blocked by the unfair mercantile system of the past.

The global community has a make or break opportunity, as it gathers in Bali for the 13th Conference of the Parties of the UN Framework Convention on Climate Change, to put into motion a stronger, and more effective, regime to address climate change. The outcomes from the Bali conference will be crucial in determining whether environmental space and the development policy choice for developing countries will be enhanced or foreclosed. The developing countries must work together to ensure that a clear and well-articulated development agenda is incorporated as a central component into the post-2012 global climate policy regime.

Mindful of the global challenge that affects the whole of humanity and not just the people of the South, the South Centre will provide both a forum to discuss these issues and technical expertise to the developing countries in their quest for a legitimate share in the resources available for development.

Why is a proper analysis of the current food crisis so important?

1 June 2008

Global food prices have been rising steadily since 2002, including 65 per cent since January 2008. Global hot spots of unrest caused by spiralling food prices in the last few months include Burkina Faso, Cameroon, Egypt, Haiti, Indonesia, Ivory Coast, Mauritania, Mozambique and Senegal.

The UN special rapporteur on the right to food, Jean Ziegler, reported in March this year that despite real growth in some countries of the South, overall there has been little progress in reducing the number of victims of hunger and malnutrition. Hunger has *increased* every year since 1996, reaching an estimated 854 million people despite commitments made to halve it at the 2000 Millennium Summit and the 2002 World Food Summit.

Among the most popular suggested causes of the food crisis are:

- Global warming that has disrupted the balance of the natural systems of air, water and weather patterns essential for food production
- Rising fuel prices pushing up the cost of, for example, fertilisers and transport
- Conversion of food land to biofuels
- Increased consumption by rising middle classes in, for example, India and China
- Dismantling of agricultural infrastructure in countries in the South that during 1980s and 1990s followed the structural adjustment policies of the Bretton Woods institutions
- US farm policy
- US and EU subsidies – including the practice of 'shifting boxes' in order to maintain subsidies, and EU common agricultural policy reform
- Financial speculation in the food sector.

Before going deeper into an analysis of any of the above, it is necessary to tread the jungle of probable causes warily, for one could tread on sensitive toes. The issue is not only 'hot on the streets', it is also 'hot in the boardrooms'. Jacques Diouf, the director-general of the United Nations Food and Agriculture Organisation (FAO), was treading carefully through this jungle when, in describing the spiralling food prices as an 'emergency', he blamed both the developing and the developed countries as sources of the crisis. In the developing countries, he said, it was, among other factors, the steady migration of rural populations to the cities and adverse weather conditions. In the developed countries it was, among others, the diversion of farmland to produce biofuels and speculation in the futures markets.

So, how do we traverse this jungle? In our view, there are five basic guidelines, or principles, which must form the basis of any food policy. These are:

1. *The principle of food sovereignty* This is not the same as 'food security'. A country can have food security through food imports. Dependence on food imports is precarious and prone to multiple risks – from price risks, to supply risks, to conditionality risks (policy conditions that come with food imports). Food sovereignty, on the other hand, implies ensuring domestic production and supply of food. It means that the nationals of the country (or at the very least nationals within the region) must primarily be responsible for ensuring that the nation and the region are first and foremost dependent on their own efforts and resources to grow their basic foods.
2. *The principle of priority of food over export* Crops produced by small farms should be sustained by state provision of the necessary infrastructure of financial credit, water, energy, extension service, transport, storage, marketing, and insurance against crop failures due to climate changes or other unforeseen circumstances.
3. *The principle of self-reliance and national ownership and control over the main resources for food production* These are land, seeds, water, energy, essential fertilisers and technology and equipment (for production, harvesting, storage and transport).
4. *The principle of food safety reserves* Each nation must maintain, through primarily domestic production and storage systems (including village storage as well as national silos) sufficient stocks of reserve foods to provide for emergencies.

5. *The principle of a fair and equitable distribution of reserve foods* During emergencies, food must be shared among the population fairly and equitably.

Sadly, and with dire consequences, these quite commonsensical and, we believe, reasonable principles, have not been followed by many governments in the South. They have been grossly violated in five principal ways, in addition to other minor ones:

1. *Distorted state policies on production and trade* (e.g. removal of tariffs that made local producers vulnerable to imported food from rich countries that subsidised their own food production and exports)
2. *Land grabs by rich commercial farmers*, thus disempowering small producers and rendering them vulnerable to 'market attacks'
3. *Effective loss of control over food production resources*, including land (even where nationals 'owned' land) because of imported seeds, imported fertilisers, imported machinery, imported technical assistance and imported banks, and also loss of control over water and energy as a result of the surrender by states of these resources to foreign corporations in hope of benefiting from foreign direct investment (FDI)
4. *Donor aid dependence*, and bad advice that came with it from donors, including the World Bank and the IMF, during the heyday of the Washington consensus (1975–2005)
5. *Disruption of the infrastructure of food production* as a consequence of the previous four factors.

Many countries have, as a result, lost their food sovereignty. They have become cash crop or mineral exporters, lost control of the resources needed for production (land, water, seeds, energy, technology, etc), and have become dependent on food imports, not only during periods of emergency, but also in 'normal' times.

Here are a few examples of these 'existential truth' of our times. It is estimated that up to 15 million Mexican farmers and their families (in particular indigenous peoples) may have been displaced from their livelihoods as a result of the North American Free Trade Agreement (NAFTA) and competition with subsidised American maize.

Just ten corporations, including Aventis, Monsanto, Pioneer and Syngenta, control one-third of the $23 billion commercial seed market and 80 per cent of the $28 billion global pesticide market. Another ten corporations, including Cargill, control 57 per cent of the total sales of the world's leading 30 retailers and account for 37 per cent of the revenues earned by the world's top 100 food and beverage companies.

In an increasingly liberalising (globalising) world, transnational corporations (TNCs) have increased their control over the supply of water, especially in the South. In many cases, private sector participation in water services has been one of the aid conditionalities of the so-called donor assistance (ODAs) from donor countries, the IMF and the World Bank. Just three companies, Veolia Environnement (formerly Vivendi Environnment), Suez Lyonnaise des Eaux and Bechtel (USA), control a majority of private water concessions globally.

The biofuels industry is inherently predatory on land and resources, especially if it is generated out of food crops such as maize and soya beans. It is estimated that producing 50 litres of biofuels to run a car for a one-day trip or three days around town would consume about 200kg of maize – enough to feed one person for a year. This does not even take into account the cost of energy, water and other resources that go into biofuel's production.

The Social Enterprise Development (SEND) Foundation in Ghana have criticised multinational companies that are trying, using the food crisis, to capture African agriculture through the so-called Green Revolution for Africa. FoodFirst Information and Action Network (FIAN) said that peasants have been evicted in several African countries so that palm oil can be produced from forests.

The heavy production and export subsidies that OECD countries grant their farmers – more than $349 billion in 2006 or almost $1 billion per day – mean that subsidised European fruit, vegetables, lower grade meat and chicken wings can be found in markets all over West Africa at lower prices than local produce.

A proper analysis of the food crisis is a matter that cannot be left to trade negotiators, investment experts, or agricultural engineers. It is essentially a matter of political economy. A crisis for some is an opportunity for others. Any analysis of the present food crisis carries with it its own prescription, and these prescriptions have the potential to bring benefits for some and losses for others.

The analytical jungle needs to be carefully traversed. But in this jungle, watch out for animals that have sharp claws and powerful teeth. We thought imperialism was a dirty word not to be uttered in polite company. But under the title 'Food Investment, not Imperialism', an editorial in the London *Financial Times* of 13 May 2008 advocated foreign investments as a solution to the problem of food crisis. However, having expounded on the virtue of what it called 'cross-border farm investment' (read, FDIs), it goes on with what we cannot but agree. It says:

> The only exception is if investment in agriculture turns into imperialism. That is a practice with a long and unpleasant history, from the plantation agriculture of the European empires to the 1954 coup in Guatemala, assisted by the US Central Intelligence Agency, at least in part for the benefit of the United Fruit Company. A developing country can suffer if capital intensive cash crops are produced at the expense of labour intensive food.

Bravo! Wisdom sometimes comes through looking at history with hindsight. Sadly, history is often forgotten by those who are in a hurry to sign free trade agreements, economic partnership agreements, donor aid loans and grants, and bilateral investment treaties. The lure of money to balance the budget or to finance food imports is too powerful against the lessons of history. If only our policy makers were able to exercise some foresight!

Global food crisis: alternatives to the green revolution

1 July 2008

In June 2008 the South Centre, in conjunction with the mission of Indonesia in Geneva, organised a one-day workshop on the food and energy crisis stalking the world. Central to the food crisis is the issue of prices. How are high prices in food and energy sources going to affect their production and distribution? The second question is: Who are the likely beneficiaries of high food prices?

All food commodities go through a long chain of value additions from the direct producers to the final consumers. With rice, for example, there are the direct producers (the tillers of the soil, more often than not women); suppliers of inputs (seeds, energy, fertilisers and water); machinery suppliers (tractors and harvesters); providers of storage and transport; banks and credit institutions that provide seasonal credit and finance; insurance companies; millers, grinders and bakers; exporters, shipping agents and shippers; and, of course, government officials that control and regulate the chain. When food prices rise, all these stakeholders expect a higher return for their own contributions to the long production and distribution chain.

We know from historical experience that those that control capital (money and credit) and the market (domestic and export) are the ones that usually take the lion's share of a hike in prices. These are global food corporations, domestic exporters linked with foreign corporations, bankers and shippers, and millers that have the capacity to purchase grain and hold it in silos until prices rise. Usually, it is the direct producers – the cultivators – who lose out because of their fragmentation and weak bargaining position. If production is mechanised and capitalised, then the rural workers, small farmers and peasants also lose out – as happened, for example, in the Punjab during India's 'green revolution'. The losers also include ordinary consumers – both urban and rural – unless there are means to compensate them for higher prices (e.g. through subsidies or price controls).

In other words, the hike in food prices comes with mixed blessings – an opportunity for some but misery for most. So the big question is: How is the recent hike in food prices going to pan out? Who is going to profit, and who stands to lose?

At the June workshop, one speaker said that while the sudden escalation of food prices in recent months is deplorable – because of the suffering it causes to poor people without the means to purchase food from the market – high food prices provide an opportunity for capital to return to profitable investment in agriculture. What we may be witnessing soon, he said, is a 'renaissance' for the agricultural sector. There are two aspects to his argument.

The first is that the high fuel costs are likely to be an enduring feature of the global commodities market. We are moving from a pre-bioenergy world to a post-bioenergy world. The traditional ways in which food was grown have to be adjusted to this new situation.

The second is that for far too long investment in agriculture has been parsimonious. It has declined over the years because investors can get better returns on their capital from other sectors of the global economy. With the price hike in food, this could change.

We view this global corporate strategy with trepidation. In our view, high food prices might trigger an agricultural renaissance for global corporations, but it is unlikely to benefit the poor of the world. As we pointed out in the previous editorial, just ten corporations control 57 per cent of the total sales of the world's leading 30 retailers and account for 37 per cent of the revenues earned by the world's top 100 food and beverage companies. Others that are likely to prosper from this anticipated renaissance are corporate producers of seeds, fertilisers, pesticides and biofuels, and those that control access and distribution of water. They have benefited from all previous 'green revolutions' sparked off by food crises. It is no wonder that corporations and intergovernmental organisations that hold the market as the solution to all problems have welcomed the price hikes, and are now propagating the idea, among others, of a green revolution for Africa.

By contrast to this global corporate model, the mission of Thailand presented a paper on how the country has been dealing with the issue of food and energy security. There are essentially three pillars to their strategy.

The first is national and regional self-reliance for the production of basic staple foods. In the case of Thailand, in 2007 they produced 16.9 million tons (MT) of rice for domestic consumption and 13.3MT for export; 27.4MT of cassava, of which 8.6MT was for domestic consumption and the rest for export; and 1.4MT of palm oil, mostly for domestic consumption. It produced most of its requirement for corn, but did import a certain amount.

Second is the centrality of small farmers in food production. Thailand encourages small farmers and, to this end, the government provides the necessary infrastructure of support to the farmers – R&D for new rice varieties, water resources (irrigation, dams and reservoirs), extension services to encourage good agricultural practices, and development of new value-added products, including organic food for niche foreign markets.

The last is regional cooperation. Modelled after the Organisation of Oil Exporting Countries (OPEC), Thailand floated the idea of an Organisation of Rice Exporting Countries (OREC), consisting of five countries (Thailand, Vietnam, China, India and Pakistan). However, implementing the idea has met with some challenges. Nonetheless, since 2005 Thailand has actively cooperated with Vietnam, with which it shares information, R&D and other ways to limit competition in the global market.

The model of building on national and regional collective self-reliance has the advantage that major decisions on food production and distribution are controlled by nationals and not by some remote corporations simply because they have the capital. However, in this national or regional strategy, the struggle to gain a fair share of the price still remains. It shifts largely between the direct producers (the tillers), the middlemen (input suppliers, transporters, millers, bakers, etc) and the consumers.

Equity demands a fair sharing between these three. Here the role of the state is critical. In our view, a greater share of the hike in prices should go into the pockets of the tillers and rural households. Why? For four reasons:

1. Increasing the capacity for rural self-sustenance also helps to stop the rural–urban drift
2. Retaining a higher share of the total value of production in the rural areas also helps build rural services, especially in health and education
3. Higher incomes in the pockets of the rural masses encour-

ages the production of other basic necessities on which peasants, small farmers and their households spend their income: clothes, shoes, bicycles, two-band radios, refrigerators, etc. It is these, and not the production of, for example, luxury cars for export that expand the domestic market and provide opportunities for decent employment

4. A satisfied, literate and healthy rural population and urban working class are good for democracy.

In view of the above, the countries of the South have to balance between the immediate demands of the moment and planning for the long-term strategy. Clearly, there is some urgency about the present crisis situation. Communities in distress will need emergency supplies of food. Farmers facing the next agricultural season will need the necessary inputs: credit, extension advice, guaranteed floor prices, storage and transport facilities and marketing outlets. Governments that are facing these immediate challenges should negotiate for food relief aid and grants to meet emergency needs. Donors and intergovernmental organisations such as the World Food Programme can effectively supply the necessary emergency food aid provided there are no policy conditionalities attached. Before turning for help from outside, countries must first see what they can do within their national and regional domains. The long-term strategy is a different matter. Here, they should plan on the basis of the direct participation of direct producers, peasants and small farmers. Equity demands that they are better rewarded than has happened in the past with previous hikes in food price.

5

Putting trade into perspective

Introduction

The Doha round of trade negotiations which started in 2001 were aimed at further liberalisation of trade with a development bias. The outcome document of the Doha round has 20 chapters, of which the most important are on agriculture, industry and services. All issues for negotiations have a political, a social and an economic dimension. But while industry is primarily economic and services are primarily social, agriculture is primarily political. How so? This is the question raised in the first essay, 'Some home truths about current negotiations on agriculture at WTO'.

In the next essay, 'A paradox of trade and development', we draw attention to the flower industry, taking Kenya as an example. Growers draw water out of Lake Naivasha on an average of approximately 20,000m³ a day in order to grow flowers to export to Europe. At this rate, in another 50 years the lake will shrink to a muddy pool of dead water. To protect its flower market in Europe Kenya felt compelled, along with other countries, to initial the signing of an economic partnership agreement (EPA) with the European Union. This ceremony was being performed at the same time as, 10,000 miles away in Bali, Indonesia, countries were discussing the effects of climate change and global warming on, among other things, food security, access to water and the means of sustaining basic livelihood in the South. What should be Kenya's priority: the protection of the water of Lake Naivasha or the export of flowers to Europe?

The editorial 'EPAs will benefit Europe to the cost of both ACP and Latin American countries' analyses the EPA agreements between the African, Caribbean and Pacific (ACP) countries and the European Union. Among other things it argues that the EPAs are creating divisions among ACP regions, and also jeopardising their regional economic integration. It is the old divide and rule strategy of the empire.

This strategy is daily played out in the workings of the World Trade Organisation, and even in its older sister organisation, the United Nations Conference on Trade and Development. In 'Reflections on UNCTAD XII' we draw attention to a clear bias in the working out of the trading system. At the UNCTAD XII gathering in Accra, the private sector (in the guise of the World Investment Forum) was seamlessly integrated into the official deliberations, but civil society was largely marginalised. This was in April 2008. By the time the year ended, the private sector companies in the US and in other countries were going cap in hand to their states to bale them out of bankruptcies. The private sector is self-indulgent and speaks loudly only when it is making profits. For UNCTAD, however, its natural ally is the people and the civil society through which the people speak.

Some home truths about current negotiations on agriculture at WTO

1 October 2007

The Doha negotiating mandate has 20 chapters, of which the most important are on agriculture, industry and services. All the issues for negotiation have political, social, and economic implications for developing countries.

History and economic logic both show that no country can develop and improve the standard of living of its people without industry and manufacturing. The WTO negotiations on Non-Agricultural Market Access (NAMA) are therefore crucial. If trade negotiators from the developing countries get their industrial tariff coefficients wrong (i.e. the parameters to define the extent of tariff reductions to be undertaken after the Doha negotiations), industrialisation of their countries will probably not occur. In the case of services, if they underestimate the importance of their social dimension, then negotiators from the South will have a lot to answer for if their countries lose national control over health, education, transport, banking and other services. And, if agriculture negotiations go wrong, food security and the livelihood of millions of people will be jeopardised.

In the case of agriculture, there is a huge difference between the North and the South. The difference is that, in the South, agriculture is not simply an issue related to commercial or trade concerns. It is a basic livelihood issue. While in the North between 3 and 5 per cent of the population live off agriculture, the figures in the South range from 40 to 80 percent. If trade negotiators from the North make mistakes in agricultural negotiations, they jeopardise the lifestyles of the few currently benefiting from the system of support to agriculture. If, on the other hand, the trade negotiators from the South make mistakes, they put at stake the livelihood of tens of millions of people. Simply put, for the North, agriculture is a 'protectionist' issue for a select and privileged few (in many cases agro-industrial corporations, especially in the United States); for most of the South, it is fundamentally a livelihood and developmental issue. This is the most important home truth about current agricultural negotiations in the WTO.

The following pointers are made in the spirit of advising caution and prudence to developing country negotiators with respect to the agriculture negotiations.

First, the development dimension must incorporate special and differential treatment and proportionality in the level of commitments between developed and developing countries. The diversity of situations among developing countries must be recognised by allowing differentiation in commitments depending on members' capacity and levels of development.

Second, real concessions in market access by developing countries should not be exchanged in return for paper cuts in subsidies by the industrialised world. The US offer to reduce trade-distorting subsidies to agriculture down to $17 billion still significantly leaves space for this country to increase support to agriculture from current levels. A similar situation will exist for the EU if the negotiations settle around the numbers proposed by the chairman of the negotiating groups in his draft modalities text of 17 July.[1]

Moreover, everything seems to indicate that the criteria related to permitted subsidies – the so called green box measures – will remain mostly untouched, providing an escape clause to further increase subsidies to agriculture in the future, with no restraint. Finally, a renewal of the peace clause – a provision in the current agriculture agreement which imposed restraint on members wanting to attack agriculture subsidies through dispute settlement procedures or countervailing measures – as requested by the United States will further undermine reform to the disadvantage of developing countries.

Third, developing country negotiators should not lose sight of the overall development approach to the negotiations. If the path towards balanced development is through the diversification of an economy from the production of commodities to manufacturing and services industries, and adding value across the whole economy, commitments in NAMA and services must be seen in this broader context in order to avoid compromising on options for the future development of an economy.

Appropriate development-oriented reform of the rules governing the global trade system, particularly in agriculture, is necessary. But such reform, and the measurement of success in achieving such reform, must be made against the development benchmarks provided by the Doha ministerial declaration. Content should not be sacrificed to the political imperatives of certain members. The major trading partners, primary beneficiaries of the current multilateral trading system, need to show leadership and make the necessary concessions leading to a successful conclusion of a truly development-oriented outcome to the Doha negotiations.

Note

1. See South Centre's comments on the draft modalities at: http://www.southcentre.org/publications/AnalyticalNotes/Agriculture/2007Aug_Comments_Draft_Modalities.pdf

A paradox of trade and development

16 December 2007

Events unfold odd paradoxes that at first are unthinkable, but become obvious on deeper reflection.

Two simultaneous events unfolded in recent weeks. One was the initialled, goods-only interim agreement leading to a full economic partnership agreement (EPA) between the countries of Eastern Africa and the European Union (EU) some time in 2008. The second was the 13th Conference of the Parties (COP 13) of the United Nations Framework Convention on Climate Change at Bali in Indonesia: two events with no immediately obvious, compelling connection.

The essence of the EPA between Eastern Africa and the EU was to restructure the economic relations between Eastern Africa and the EU on the principle of reciprocity, so that the two clearly unequal 'partners' begin trading as though they are 'equal' partners. The Eastern African countries did not have to sign the EPA; they did have other options, but they signed it. There were several factors behind the signing of the agreement. One of these, from the East African side, was safeguarding the export interest of horticulturalists in Kenya. It was argued that with the end of the EU preferential system on 1 January 2008, they would face increased tariffs in the European market and so perhaps lose out to competitors from other flower-growing countries of the South. The market, it was argued, had to be secured.

Bali was a conference essentially about the effects of climate change. From the perspective of the South, it was about the effects of global warming and the increasing use of energy on, among other things, food security, access to water, and the means of sustaining and improving livelihood and development prospects in the South.

What went unnoticed at Bali was the connection between the EPA agreement just signed by the East African countries and climate change. It is about 10,000km as the crow flies from Bali to Lake Naivasha in Kenya. Naivasha is Europe's major source of cut flowers. The UK alone imported 18,000 tons of flowers from Kenya last year, up from about 10,000 tons in 2001. The flower growers draw water out of the lake on an average of approximately 20,000m^3 a day. Lake Naivasha is dying. Officially 130km^2, it shrank last year to about 75 per cent of its 1982 size. At this rate, in another 50 years it will shrink to a muddy pool of dead water. The papyrus swamps that were the breeding grounds for fish have gone, even as the labouring population in the flower farms is increasing. People are facing severe problems of food and water insecurity.

Given the amount of water that goes into flower production, one could say that water is exported from Kenya to Europe in the form of flowers. While lovers in Europe will celebrate their Christmas by exchanging roses and carnations, people around Lake Naivasha may have no bread, and certainly no fish. Bali and Lake Naivasha are 10,000km apart as the crow flies, practically on the same latitude. But the crow may have failed to carry the message of the people of Naivasha. Did anybody hear the cry of the peasants and fisher folk of Lake Naivasha at Bali? Or at Brussels? Or, even nearer at home, in Kampala where the EPA agreement was signed?

EPAs will benefit Europe to the cost of both ACP and Latin American countries

16 June 2008

Currently, the African, Caribbean and Pacific (ACP) countries are locked in negotiations with the European Union (EU) over the economic partnership agreements (EPAs), as part of the implementation of the Cotonou Agreement that was signed in June 2000.

Initially, when the EPA negotiations began in 2001 there was going to be just one agreement. It was to be between the then 15 countries of Europe, and 76 of the ACP countries. Since then the EU has enlarged itself to 27 members still signing as one entity with full powers given to the European Commission (EC) to negotiate for all of them. The ACP countries in the meantime have allowed themselves to be fragmented into three regions (Africa, Caribbean and the Pacific); then, later, into six (Western Africa, Central Africa, Eastern Africa, Southern Africa, the Caribbean and the Pacific); and later still into several — in the case of Africa, into its almost total fragmentation. Finally, we now have, in many cases, bilateral agreements between one African country on one side and the European Community on the other – a veritable David and Goliath phenomenon. It is tempting to make the comparison with the Berlin Conference of 1884, when European imperial powers sat around a map of Africa and carved it out between them. However, there are two significant differences.

First, Africans are at the table, some of them signing asymmetrical agreements, compelled by the compulsion of perceived circumstances that leave them, they believe, no other option.

Second, in 1884, the European imperial powers were competing with one another for Africa's resources. Now Europe is united under one banner in competition with the United States, Japan and now with the emerging trading giants like India and China.

What does Europe want out of the EPAs? It wants, primarily, to cement and secure:

* A historically created relationship euphemistically called 'partnership' in order to ensure that it has competitive access to the raw materials of ACP countries, especially oil and minerals

- Market access for European goods, but in particular market access for services, such as financial services, communications and consultancies, especially if these can be tied in with aid from Europe
- A slice of the market in government procurement, which in some countries can be as much as 50 per cent of the national budget
- Opportunities for investment for European corporations in the ACP countries
- A market for its products protected by means of intellectual property (IP) rights because it is losing a competitive edge over supply of goods through competition from countries like China.

The last item is crucially important for Europe. Why? Because, secured IP rights will provide the Europeans with a protected market in the ACP countries against 'counterfeits' from China and the other emerging markets. Combine this with the vigorous efforts Europe is making to obtain SECURE – Standards Employed by Customs for Uniform Rights Enforcement and it is clear why the Europeans are in such a hurry to conclude the EPAs. The competition from China, India, Brazil and other so-called 'emerging' economies is knocking at the door. Further delay would whittle away Europe's competitive edge in Africa.

What is the ACP getting in return? The answer is the promise of continued 'secure' access to the European market in the hope, perhaps, that a revised formula of Rules of Origin will improve market entry; and the guarantee of financial resources from the European Development Fund (EDF).

Both, in our view, are of dubious value. The competitiveness of ACP products in the EU market will come under increasing pressure as the EU concludes a series of free trade agreements with other countries (India, ASEAN, Andean countries, Central American countries, etc). Moreover, some non-ACP countries (such as those in Latin America) may resent what they will see as unfair discrimination against them. In solidarity with our Latin friends, we would agree that this is indeed unfair. One group of developing countries is pitted against another group of developing countries. It is difficult to escape the image of dogs fighting for the bone thrown in their middle.

As for the EDF, it will lose value because of the conditionalities attached to aid, including 'tied aid'. Europe may chip in a bit more in the form of 'Aid for Trade' (although there are serious doubts that it will), and in 'trade facilitation' (so far an untouched subject in the negotiations). Besides, it now seems certain that the resources possibly available will, in any event, not match the costs that the implementation of and adjustment to these agreements will generate.

There are several problems with the interim EPAs, of which the following three are critical. First, the EPAs are creating divisions among ACP regions to the extent of jeopardising regional economic integration. In fact, the Cotonou Agreement envisaged regional integration of the ACP countries *prior* to the EPAs. This, apparently, has been now reversed. Interim EPAs have established, perhaps in an irreversible manner, a *reverse sequencing* – preferences for Europe first, and only then for neighbouring countries in the region.

Second, the concessions made within these agreements are greater – both in extent and scope – than those that would have been required to ensure their basic conformity with WTO norms. Third, despite the controversy over the need to negotiate trade-related disciplines (e.g. the Singapore issues) and trade in services, the interim agreements tie ACP countries to a detailed and intensive negotiating agenda on these issues.

With the end of the December 2007 deadline (when the Doha waiver on EPAs lapsed) the issue of the waiver has become obsolete. There is no longer a need for the ACP countries to rush through the negotiations in 2008. Nonetheless, the ACP countries are being pressed to sign the EPAs. You do not need a nuclear physicist to say that the EPAs are totally asymmetrical and unfair.

Another issue is the cost of the imposed EPA agreement on the development of the ACP countries. A study by the United Nations Economic Commission for Africa (UNECA) shows that African countries would stand to lose $1.9 billion in tariff revenue, and another study by the Commonwealth Secretariat estimates that over 10 years the ACP countries would need an additional sum of €9.2 billion for a minimum level of restructuring adjustment.

EPAs are too serious a matter to leave to technical trade experts. Though important, the arguments cannot be reduced to mere technicalities. There is a larger political dimension that the political leaders of ACP countries and the EU should take seriously. This is the issue of equity and historical justice. Both the EU and the ACP countries have pushed this issue under the rug for the sake of peace and practicality. But in doing so, they are closing their eyes to grave historical injustice done to the peoples of the ACP regions. Let us recall certain aspects of this historical legacy:

- A built-in, structural 'division of labour' based on the ACP countries providing human beings in the form of commodities, super-exploited wage labour and grossly under-priced natural resources. These were needed for the industrialisation of Europe from the 17th to the 20th centuries
- Europe's comparative advantage in manufactured products, equipment, services (such as shipping, insurance and banking) and IP products arising out of this historical division of labour
- The ensuing liberation struggle (from the end of the First World War to the liberation of South Africa in 1994), at enormous cost, especially to people in Africa, from which they have not yet fully recovered
- The Cotonou and previous agreements that cemented a colonial and asymmetrical relationship.

The people of Latin America are correct in challenging the EPAs, for these are indeed discriminatory. Trade preferences must go, of course. They are an insult to the dignity of ACP peoples, who do not (should not) want to be treated as less than equal. But deeply embedded, structured relationships created over 300 years of history cannot simply be broken in 50 or 60 years. They cannot be broken, in any case, until the erstwhile colonies have put in place a proper exit strategy from aid dependence – a project on which the South Centre is currently working. The people in Latin America should know that they and ACP countries are all in the same historical boat, and the destination called 'development' has not yet been reached.

In the meantime, the question must be asked: Who should bear the cost of this historical legacy? It is a bigger question than simply the €1.5 billion in tariff revenue loss and the €9.2 billion in 'adjustment costs'. It is a question of historical justice. We are of the view that the European Union has the responsibility to compensate the ACP countries for any losses they suffer as a result of a forcible adjustment to a new trade regime out of the historically dependent relationship created by Europe with its former colonies. This is not 'development aid'. It is a requirement to rebalance rights and obligations towards a more honest partnership agreement. It is the moral and legitimate entitlement of ACP countries.

Reflections on UNCTAD XII

1 May 2008

Earlier, in chapter 2, in the editorial 'Why strengthening UNCTAD is also in the interest of the North' we argued why it was in the interest of both the North as well as the South to strengthen and recreate the United Nations Conference on Trade and Development (UNCTAD) as a forum where issues of concern can be addressed in a proper manner. Attempts to take matters outside of the United Nations (UN), such as at G7/8 meetings or at the World Economic Forum, have not been inclusive or democratic. The UN, with all its weaknesses, is still the only multilateral, intergovernmental, democratic institution the world has, and UNCTAD is part of that machinery. Overhaul it if necessary, but do not reduce its capacity to address issues of trade and development, which was its original mandate.

Unfortunately, UNCTAD seems to have been further compromised in Accra. Once the UNCTAD secretariat and others concerned have analysed the final outcome document, the extent of the damage wil be clearer. For now, it looks like UNCTAD has lost the ground it had partially recovered at UNCTAD XI in Sao Paulo.

The countries of the North appeared in Accra to want to diminish UNCTAD as much as they could. Even those among them that normally favour the UN's multilateralism were bent on reducing UNCTAD rather than empowering it. In the anodyne language of UN diplomacy, UNCTAD should 'not do everything' but should 'focus' on what it was best at. In other words, UNCTAD should leave matters of trade to the World Trade Organisation (WTO) and finances to the Bretton Woods institutions and the Organisation for Economic Cooperation and Development (OECD). The result was that major trade and finance issues in the development agenda were amputated from the body politic of UNCTAD. Its disfigured and mutilated body was then left with essentially the task of research and the provision of technical assistance to the countries of the South on residual matters such as aid for trade.

Is this a gradual denouement of UNCTAD, a carefully sequenced demise leading to its ultimate collapse at the next Conference in 2012? Possibly, but not inevitably.

Strengthening and recreating UNCTAD is not a bureaucratic act; it is a political act. Only its members can build it or destroy it. What we need – and this is becoming ever more urgent – is a redefinition of what constitutes 'membership'. In diplomatic parlance, only states are members of intergovernmental organisations. However, we have moved some distance from this Westphalian definition of the interstate system. Increasingly, non-state actors, among them the private sector and civil society, are recognised agents of international discourse. And this is where the UNCTAD secretariat could have done more than it did in the months and years between UNCTAD XI and XII.

At Accra itself, UNCTAD did set up the World Investment Forum (WIF) for the private sector and a separate forum for the civil society. The difference, however, was that the private sector was better integrated into the official deliberations than civil society. High-powered speakers, including the representatives of finance capital, were brought centre stage and seamlessly integrated into the mainstream deliberations, whereas civil society was treated as largely marginal to the proceedings. 'Give them a tent and email facilities, and keep them happy' appeared to be the underlying philosophy of UNCTAD towards civil society. If UNCTAD had been listening carefully, it would have learnt that it was from the civil society tent in Accra that the strongest voices were raised to defend the policy space occupied by UNCTAD. This also came out clearly in the South Centre-organised informal meeting with the CSO representatives on the sides of the main event.

How does one explain this differential treatment of the private sector and civil society? There could be many explanations: for example, preceding the conference the private sector may have been better organised than global civil society. But there is more to it than that. Underlying UNCTAD's present philosophy is the oft-repeated mantra that 'the private sector is the engine of growth', while civil society are 'anti-globalisers'. Simplified, rhetorical propositions sometimes acquire the force of axiomatic truths.

One can fairly discuss the merits and demerits of the private sector and civil society without being dogmatic about either. But to treat the private sector as central to UNCTAD's discourse and civil society as marginal was doing disservice to UNCTAD itself, and ultimately to its own attempt to regain its past glory. Why?

Because once you identify the private sector, and especially private capital flows and foreign direct investments (FDIs) as the engine of growth, you automatically shift responsibility out of the hands of UNCTAD and into those that are better qualified to deal with matters of finance and investments, such as the Bretton Woods institutions, the WTO, the United Nations Industrial Development Organisation (UNIDO), the OECD and, not accidentally, the World Association of Investment Promotion Agencies (WAIPA), which organised the WIF at UNCTAD XII. The only speaker who seriously interrogated the underlying assumptions of the other WIF speakers at the podium was Benjamin Mkapa, President Emeritus of the United Republic of Tanzania.

The private sector has a role, no doubt, but so does civil society. Civil society has the role of providing a window to the existential truth about the reality on the ground as it affects the poor. For example, the official discourse in the main forum raised the alarm about the looming food crisis, but it was at the civil society forum that its structural as well as immediate causes were analysed. At the civil society forum there was anguished discussion, to give another example, of the seriously flawed economic partnership agreements (EPAs) between the European Union and the African, Caribbean and Pacific (ACP) countries, but, alas, the main forum was completely oblivious to this.

UNCTAD may work with the private sector, but its natural ally is civil society, whose focus is real life, the huge gap between growth which UNCTAD (and mainstream ideology) presumes will automatically flow from private investments – and development, which civil society argues can only come when people are empowered to take their destiny in their own hands.

This came starkly to the fore on the issue of the looming food crisis. For the private sector this presents an opportunity to push for 'green revolution' for Africa, with commercialised agriculture. For civil society, it poses a challenge to bring about necessary land reform and create proper institutional structures (such as credit facilities and extension services) to the ordinary peasant farmers so that they, and not agricultural corporations, are responsible for bringing food to the table of the hungry. Sadly, UNCTAD missed an opportunity to offer the International Assessment of Agricultural Knowledge, Science and Technology for Development (IAASTD) to present its report to the conference. The recently released report, a work of 400 scientific experts, criticised the present trade and the intellectual property (IP) regimes as favouring the rich and the rich countries to the detriment of the poor. It criticised GMO-based agriculture, and advocated safeguarding natural resources and agro-ecological practices and indigenous knowledge systems in agriculture. The report was vehemently opposed by global agricultural corporations and some large countries which are home to these corporations. If UNCTAD failed to provide space to the IAASTD at Accra, it might have been an oversight, but for the poor it was a costly oversight.

If ever an argument was needed for UNCTAD to better use the medium of civil society to advance its development agenda, it was Accra that provided it. There was plenty in the activities of civil society just across from the official main forum that could have provided the ammunition to UNCTAD to inject new life into itself. Sadly, a chasm separated the negotiating context of UNCTAD (seeking to arrive at some diplomatic truth about reality) from the civil society forum that was expressing the brutal reality of existential truth. What the official discourse lacked, the society provided, but the twain did not meet.

6

Ending aid dependence

Introduction

The main story line in official literature and in the mainstream media is that despite everything the developing countries are doing well, and that the Millennium Development Goals (MDGs) are 'by and large' on target. This is a big lie. A certain lack of candor characterises the present development dialogue between the rich and the poor nations. There is a palpable reluctance to accept the truth that the system is not working for the poor of the world. In 'Development dialogue with donors', we draw attention to six issues for debate:

1. Globally, the subservience of the development agenda to the trade liberalisation agenda and market fundamentalism
2. Within the UN system, the subservience of development to, primarily, the security and economic concerns of the North
3. The dominance of the North in global institutions of knowledge creation and policy direction for the South, backed by promises of aid
4. The locked-in condition in which the bulk of the South trades at the lower end of the value-added production chain
5. The de-industrialisation of large numbers of countries of the South
6. The threat of North-dominated 'regionalism' to the integrity and survival of smaller countries of the South.

The theme of aid dependence is raised more specifically in the essay 'Ending aid dependence'. For far too long, the debate on development aid has been constrained by conceptual traps and the limitations of the definitions provided by the donors. If the recipients or beneficiaries of aid are to own the process, as present trends in the development literature suggest, then the conceptual reframing of the issues must itself change its location from the donors to the recipients.

In the much-paraded and OECD-inspired and promoted Accra Action Agenda (AAA) on 'aid effectiveness', the donor countries somehow managed to persuade the countries of the South, in particular African countries, that their development depended on largess from the rich countries, and they had better get their governance right, as prescribed by the donor countries, in order to make aid effective. At the Accra conference in September 2008, the 1,200 assembled delegates of the aid industry somehow failed to ask the obvious question: Why are poor countries poor, and why do the rich countries continue to become richer? This is the theme of the essay on 'Assessing the Accra Action Agenda'.

This chapter concludes with a foreword by the immediate former President of Tanzania, Benjamin W. Mkapa to the book, *Ending Aid Dependence* by Yash Tandon. The former president cautioned Africa against endorsing the AAA. 'If adopted,' he says, 'it would subject the recipients to a discipline of collective control by the donors right down to the village level.'

Development dialogue with donors

16 January 2008

A certain lack of candour characterises the present development dialogue between the rich and the poor nations. There is a palpable reluctance to accept the truth that the system is not working for the poor of the world. Globally the poor have lost out, and not just in Africa. The share of benefits from global economic growth reaching the world's poorest people is actually shrinking, while they continue to bear an unfair share of the costs. Also, the creeping effects of climate change will worsen even further the condition of the poor.

According to the Basic Capabilities Index (BCI) published by Social Watch in June 2007, at the current rate of progress the universal access to a minimum set of social services will be achieved in sub-Saharan Africa only in 2108 – almost a century later than the target date (2015) set by Millennium Development Goals in 2000. Even as the poor are sinking, the official view is that whatever is happening will, 'ultimately', work out for the poor. Sections of civil society, more disposed than governments to exposing the reality on the ground, occasionally blow the whistle. By and large, however, their voices are drowned by the official Panglossian story line.

Sometimes, however, somebody in authority echoes the voice of civil society. Even as many in the Caribbean bureaucracy were celebrating the conclusion of the economic partnership agreement (EPA) between the CARIFORUM and the European Union, a revealing statement came from President Bharat Jagdeo of Guyana. He challenged those who were reluctant to admit that the region had lost out in the negotiations. The Caribbean nations had lost out, 'because all along they [the European Union] had the plan to dismantle the preferences and to basically bully the countries into meeting the deadlines we all set together but that could have been adjusted.' It was a bad deal, he said, but the region had no choice. 'I think it is time we come clean with our people in Guyana and across the region that this was the best we could have gotten out of a bad situation. I resent the characterisation that we won from these negotiations, we didn't win anything.'

The larger picture of the South's integration into neoliberal globalisation has a similar story. The official line repeated over and over is that, despite everything, the developing countries are doing well and that the MDGs are 'by and large' on target. But we must come clean in recognising the opposite reality in our dialogue on development with the donors. To be sure, some developing countries are doing well. Also, much responsibility lies with the poor economic and political governance in the many countries in the South. But Western governments are sometimes too quick to recognise outcomes of 'democratic' processes in the South that are perceived to serve their interests. Honesty demands that the links between the agonising realities in the South and the issues listed below are debated openly and candidly.

- Globally, the subservience of the development agenda to the trade agenda and market fundamentalism
- Within the United Nations system, the subservience of the development dimension to, primarily, the security concerns of the West
- The domination by the Bretton Woods Institutions and the WTO of both knowledge creation and policy frameworks in the South, backed by the traditional donors
- The locked-in condition where the bulk of the South finds itself in the lower end of the value-added production chain. This is particularly the case with Africa, but it is no less true of large economies such as China, India, Brazil and South Africa
- The de-industrialisation of large numbers of countries of the South
- The threat of North-dominated 'regionalism' to the integrity and survival of smaller countries of the South, as exemplified, for example, by the EPAs between the EU and ACP.

Unless these issues are openly and candidly debated, all talk about development is mere rhetoric.

This month the advisory body of the UN's Development Cooperation Forum (DCF) is meeting in Cairo. The DCF is still in its early years, so this is a good opportunity to define its role. In our view, the DCF must provide a normative anchor to broader issues hampering development in the South. Above all, it must not become the voice of the donors or of the OECD.

Ending aid dependence: conceptual traps of an outdated aid vocabulary

1 September 2008

For far too long the debate on development aid has been constrained by conceptual traps and the limitations of the definitions provided by the donors. If the recipients or beneficiaries of aid are to own the process, as present trends in the development literature suggest, then the conceptual reframing of the issues must move from the donors to the recipients.

The conceptual starting point is not aid but development. Growth, admittedly, is an important aspect of development; there is no need to labour the point. But growth is not the same as development. Following in the footsteps of Julius Nyerere, the founding president of Tanzania and the first chairman of the South Centre, we define development as a long democratic process that starts from within, whereby people participate in the decisions that affect their lives, without imperial interference from outside. It is aimed at improving the lives of the people and the realisation of their potential for self-support, free from fear of want and political, economic and social exploitation. As a formula it can be expressed as: Development = SF + DF - IF, where SF is the social factor (the essential well-being of the people); plus DF, the democratic factor (i.e. the right of the people to participate in the decision-making that affects their lives); minus IF the imperial factor (i.e. the right of nations to self-determination and liberation from imperial domination).

This is in sharp contrast to the mainstream orthodox economists' definition of Development as Growth + Wealth accumulation, where Growth = Open markets + Foreign investments + Good governance (as defined by the West), and the wealth accumulation by the rich is assumed to 'filter through' to the poor by market-driven forces.

Some of them, the so-called emerging economies of the South, have indeed succeeded or partly succeeded, but the bulk of the developing countries are still trapped in the shackles of history. Africa, especially, is identified as a continent that has not fared well. From this trap, Africa and others can liberate themselves only if they take matters of development into their own hands – and do not leave it to aid and its delimiting and colonising conditionalities, such as the structural adjustment programmes of the IMF and the World Bank, and now the Paris Declaration on Aid Effectiveness.

In other words, the national project, the project for self-determination, is still on the agenda of political action for developing countries. Its counter, the imperial project, is also still alive, but gradually weakening. Its ideology – the Washington Consensus and globalisation – crafted after the dominant paradigm of free market liberalism and Western systems of governance, democracy and the rule of law, has lost credibility and legitimacy. This is not to undervalue the importance of democracy or the rule of law. Without these there would be anarchy and oppression. But these values cannot be imposed on the developing countries from outside.

Ending Aid Dependence, authored by this writer,[1] provides a new and comprehensive taxonomy for development aid – in five rainbow colours. Development aid is placed along a continuum from Purple Aid (based on solidarity) on the extreme left and Red Aid (ideological aid) on the extreme right. In between are Orange Aid (which is really not aid at all, and should simply be called commercial transactions); Yellow Aid (military and political aid as explained above); and Green/Blue Aid, whose three components – the provision of global public goods (GPGs), non-tied humanitarian and emergency aid, and compensatory finance – are segments of the totality of financial, technical and technological assistance that are genuinely developmental. These are part of the global good not only from the recipient country's perspective, but also from the global perspective. One implication of this classification, for example, is that global civil society in the North as well as in the South might find they have more affinity with Purple Aid, and perhaps also with Green/Blue Aid.

The body of the book consists of seven steps that developing countries need to take in order to exit aid dependence. The most difficult is the first step – to get over the psychology of aid dependence. The dependence psychology has not only occupied the minds of leaders in many (if not most) developing countries, but it has also taken root in mass psychology. Much more can be written on the subject than is contained in the monograph. The important point is that the process has to begin somewhere and very soon. It is an agenda that has to be captured by the people themselves at community and grassroots level. However, it also requires an enlightened and visionary leadership at national, regional, and continental levels.

It is argued in the book that the present aid and development architecture at international level is an obstacle to the realisation of the national project. Three power asymmetries – of economic, political and knowledge power – are deeply embedded in the existing structures. It is a continuing battle for the developing countries to try and secure policy space within the constraints imposed by these asymmetrical structures.

The present debate on the Paris Declaration on Aid Effectiveness (PDAE) is located in this larger context to explain the circumstance in which the OECD's Development Assistance Committee (DAC) and the World Bank and the International Monetary Fund (IMF) are trying to retain their relevance and legitimacy, which have been severely eroded by the failure of their development policies, and the changing geopolitical and economic realities of the last decade or so. If the OECD, the World Bank and the IMF do not achieve what they hope for at the Accra conference on aid effectiveness (September 2008) and the Doha Monterrey Review Process (November–December 2008), then they could face oblivion within the next decade. For the DAC, its oblivion is a historical necessity in any event. At best, it should remain as a body to coordinate policies for OECD member countries. As for the World Bank and the IMF, they can salvage themselves if they pull out of Red Aid, withdraw to their original missions and give voice to those who have suffered most from the developmental failure of their policies and the financial volatility of the last two decades.

In this broad historical and political perspective, the Development Cooperation Forum (DCF) of the UN and the fast evolving South–South relationship can play a very positive role. However, the DCF faces many challenges, and its future is still largely uncertain.

At the end of the day, we need a truly heterogeneous, pluralistic global society that is based on the shared values of our civilisation and the shared fruits of the historical development of the productive forces of science, technology and human ingenuity. Only on this basis can we build a global society that is free from want, exploitation, insecurity and injustice.

Note

1. Yash Tandon (2008) *Ending Aid Dependence*, Oxford and Geneva, Fahamu and the South Centre, see www.AidExit.org.

Assessing the Accra Action Agenda

16 September 2008

The OECD-inspired and promoted Accra Action Agenda (AAA) on aid effectiveness was concluded on 4 September 2008 with a 'consensus' document by almost 1,200 delegates from about 100 countries and intergovernmental organisations (IGOs). There was also a side event of civil society organisations (CSOs) attended by some 600 delegates from 325 CSOs from 88 countries. What did Accra achieve?

What the Accra conference achieved was to draw attention to the unwieldiness of aid as an instrument of development. According to the OECD (Organisation of Economic Cooperation and Development), donors sent 15,000 missions to 54 recipient countries in 2007. In Tanzania alone the local aid bureaucracy produced 2,400 quarterly reports to donors. The Paris Declaration that formed the basis of the negotiations in Accra was aimed at bringing some order to the aid industry. *However, the irony of the situation is that the present chaotic situation of the aid industry is the second best option for the poor countries when compared to the anticipated order of the AAA.* (The best option is to get out of aid dependence.)

Why is the AAA a worse option than the present chaotic situation? Because if the AAA does get implemented, it might reduce the 15,000 missions to 5,000 and Tanzania's 2,400 quarterly reports to 400, but the process, monitoring, evaluation and sanctions would be centralised and controlled by Western aid industry bureaucrats located in the World Bank and the Development Assistance Committee (DAC) of the OECD, and the development or foreign (even defence) ministries of donor countries. Why should that be so? This is so for three reasons: one, because it is in these places where the aid industry elite are located – employing literally thousands of aid experts, country report evaluators and aid dispensers. Second, because the aid-receiving countries are fragmented and divided, and are made to believe, erroneously, that without infusions of aid from the North they will not get out of poverty. And third and most importantly, because the AAA, if it succeeds in getting off the ground, will make the really poor countries (i.e. excluding countries such as Brazil, China, India and South Africa) even more subject to the collective discipline and control of the Northern donors and the agencies they control (such as the IMF and the World Bank) than in the present chaotic situation. Indeed, if the AAA succeeds, then through bringing in say 10 or 40 per cent in the form of 'budget support', the donors could effectively control the entire budget of the recipient countries. The situation could be worse than it looks at first sight.

The Accra meeting was the biggest ever gathering on aid in history, but it failed to address or properly discuss three important questions: Why are poor countries poor? What is the ideological underpinning of the aid industry? What is the agency that would implement the AAA 'consensus'?

There was no discussion on the first issue. There was no acknowledgement of the fact that poverty is not a natural but a man-made phenomenon. It is common knowledge that poverty is created. It is created by the present system of global production, consumption and trade, which engenders the spirit of competition, selfishness and greed between nations, corporations and individuals. Two examples may suffice to illustrate the point. One is the structure of the global cotton industry. The US subsidises its cotton farmers thus lowering the price of cotton in the global market, depriving African (among other) peasant farmers of a proper price for the export of their cotton. In order that a few hundred cotton farmers in the US may continue with their subsidised affluence, a million peasants in Africa must be impoverished. The second example is so-called sensitive products – products that are sensitive to the survival of millions of peasant farmers in the developing countries. In the Doha round of trade negotiations the rich countries have demanded that in order that their agricultural and industrial producers may have access to the markets of the poor, the poor countries must limit how many products they classify as sensitive products, and therefore lower their tariffs on 'non-sensitive' products. If the rich countries have their way, it would intensify poverty in the poorest countries of the world. The Doha negotiations collapsed in July this year precisely on the issues of agricultural import surges and the need for countries to protect their producers, and cotton. For the rich it was a question of markets and for the poor a question of survival. Oddly, for countries that preach democracy and transparency the poor were not even consulted. The negotiations basically shut out the poor and their countries. Under the circumstances, it was good for the poor of the world that the negotiations collapsed.

There was no discussion in Accra of the second issue: What is the ideological content of aid? There was much talk about 'untying aid'. But this was limited to the procurement of goods and services paid for out of aid. There was no discussion about untying aid from its ideological content, what my book on *Ending Aid Dependence* classifies as 'Red Aid' – aid that is given on condition that the recipients conform to the policies of the IMF and the World Bank, the so-called Washington Consensus. What the Accra conference failed to acknowledge is that over the last 20–25 years, neoliberal globalisation has de-industrialised and now de-agriculturalised the most trade-vulnerable countries of the world. Africa, a food self-sufficient continent, is now importing food, even as food prices are skyrocketing. The argument that the best way for African countries (among others) to enter the global value chain on a competitive basis is through free trade is a self-serving ideology of those who control governance and the markets of the rich nations and their intellectual ideologues in universities and think tanks. This ideology is relentlessly pursued through the IMF, the World Bank and the World Trade Organisation. Aid or ODA (official development assistance) is one of the instruments used to enforce this ideology on the countries of the South that allow themselves to be aid dependent.

The third issue – What is the agency that would implement the AAA consensus? – was not discussed. The AAA refers to 'Ministers of developing and donor countries and Heads of multilateral and bilateral development institutions', but it appears that when it comes to monitoring and implementing the AAA, it is the OECD-created Working Party on Aid Effectiveness (WPAE) that will be the implementing agency of the AAA. At a minimum, the WPAE's composition, credentials, legitimacy, and mandate should have been debated.

It was argued earlier that the present chaotic situation in the aid industry is a second best option to the AAA, and that the best option for the countries of the South is to get out of aid dependence. To this end, the South Centre brought out its book *Ending*

Aid Dependence to coincide with the Accra conference. The publication suggests a seven-step aid exit strategy for discussion and consideration by those who are seriously contemplating ending aid dependence. It is heartening to note that some African ministers are already talking about ending aid dependence. Thus, for example, South African Finance Minister Trevor Manuel, in addressing the launch of the informal consultations on the Review of the Finance for Development process in New York on 8 September, is reported to have said: 'We should seek a world where no country is dependent on aid'.

Against this objective of ending aid dependence, the AAA is moving aid discussions in the wrong direction.

Beyond the Paris Declaration

Benjamin W. Mkapa, President of Tanzania (1995–2005)

16 September 2008

Excerpts from President Mkapa's foreword to Yash Tandon's book Ending Aid Dependence[1]

An exit strategy from aid dependence requires a radical shift both in the mindset and in the development strategy of countries dependent on aid, and the direct involvement of people in their own development. It also requires a radical and fundamental restructuring of the institutional aid architecture at the global level.

A more immediate objective is to initiate dialogue with the OECD's Paris Declaration on Aid Effectiveness,[2] which forms the basis of a high level meeting from 2 to 4 September 2008 in Accra, and to caution the developing countries against endorsing the Accra Action Agenda (AAA) offered by the OECD. If adopted, it could subject the recipients to a discipline of collective control by the donors right down to the village level. And this will especially affect the present donor-dependent countries, in particular the poorer and more vulnerable countries in Africa, Asia, Latin America and the Caribbean.

Beyond the Paris Declaration, there is still the question: what then? There has to be a strategy for ending aid dependence, to exit from it.

There are countries in the South that have more or less graduated out of aid, such as India, China, Brazil and Malaysia, and there are others which will soon self-propel themselves out of aid dependence. Aid was never a strong component in the development of either India or China. They have been reliant on their domestic savings and the development of a domestic market through the protection of local enterprises and local innovation. They have opened themselves up in recent years to the challenge of globalisation and foreign competition only after ensuring that their own markets were strong enough. Both Brazil and Malaysia have succeeded in ending their aid dependence through strong nationally oriented investment and trade policies. These included supporting and protecting the domestic market and export promotion, as well as the accompanying currency, fiscal and monetary policies.

In an earlier period, during the 1960s and 1970s, the so-called tiger economies of Korea, Singapore, Taiwan–China and Hong Kong ended their aid dependence mainly in the context of the Cold War. These countries were able to use the opportunity provided by the Cold War not only to draw substantial capital from the West, mainly the US, but also to build their production, infrastructural facilities (banking, finance, transport, communications, etc) and export capacity. They took advantage of the relatively open US market to export the products of their early manufacturing growth. They benefited from the fact that the US needed them to fight communism in that part of the world. This enabled them to initiate state-supported industrialisation without having to account to institutions such as the World Bank and the IMF, to import technology without having to pay huge fees for intellectual property rights, and to build strong reserve funds.

We are now living in a different period of history. There are countries that were neither able to take advantage of the Cold War period, nor had the benefit of a large domestic market and entrepreneurial class to develop an endogenous development strategy. We are talking about the hundred or so countries that fall within the classification of least developed countries (LDCs), the middle-income countries that are not LDCs but are still struggling to become economically independent from foreign aid, and the vulnerable, small and island economies.

The message of this book needs to be seriously considered by all those that are interested in the development of the countries of the South. If this means the rethinking of old concepts and methods of work, then let it be so.

Notes

1. Published in 2008 by the South Centre and Fahamu.
2. The Paris declaration's aid effectiveness strategy was initiated by the OECD, the Northern rich countries' think tank, in association with the World Bank.

7

The Palestine–Israel question

Introduction

On 27 December 2008, Israel launched a lethal attack on Gaza and continued the bombing for 22 days. In the end, it withdrew its forces. Israel, however, continues to retain a siege over Gaza, a narrow strip of land containing a million and half Palestinians, half of them in refugee camps living a precarious existence. Many observers are of the view that Israel's action amounted to genocide. Almost 60 years ago, before the state of Israel was created, Mahatma Gandhi wrote: 'My sympathies are all with the Jews ... But my sympathy does not blind me to the requirements of justice. The cry for the national home for the Jews does not make much appeal to me ... Palestine belongs to the Arabs in the same sense that England belongs to the English or France to the French. It is wrong and inhuman to impose the Jews on the Arabs.' In the longer piece on the subject, I argue that the Jewish problem, historically a European problem, was dumped on Palestine in 1948 by the force of arms and a resolution of the General Assembly of the United Nations when it was dominated by the North. The legitimacy of that resolution and the question of whether the British truly fulfilled their mandate to the people of Palestine must be posed again. The article argues that while the Jews have a legitimate grievance against their historical persecution, in its present predicament, the Euro-American alliance exploits the Jews in Israel, and in turn, Israel super-exploits and oppresses the Palestinians. The 'two-states solution' is primarily to serve Euro-American broader interests in the Gulf area. And one of the casualties of the war in Gaza may well be the two-state solution. What, then, is to be done? That is the question that is addressed in the essay.

The Palestine–Israel question

16 January 2009

History will not absolve those world leaders who watch with cynicism the humanitarian catastrophe unfolding in Gaza. Silence and inaction are only a step removed from complicity. The Kafkaesque contrast between Kosovo and Treblinka where the West intervened self-righteously and brought individuals to trial before the international human rights tribunals and their visible, audible connivance at the carnage now afoot in Gaza will not be lost to history. It is, surely, only a matter of time before the individuals responsible for these crimes are brought to court. Even the people of Israel, maybe the next generation, will eventually see from hindsight the ironical and cruel similarity between the concentration camps of Auschwitz and Dachau, in which many of their forefathers perished, and the 'final solution' inflicted on the ghettoized population of Gaza. Cardinal Renato Martino echoed the sentiment of Pope Benedict XVI when he compared Gaza to a Nazi camp.[1]

One casualty of the war will, surely, be the devaluation of the Jewish Holocaust. If the former victims of European persecution can do the same to the ordinary innocent women and children of another race whom they burn alive in their houses with their aerial bombing, then the lessons of the original Holocaust will be lost to history, and the Jews must tear down the temples and museums dedicated to the Holocaust. The Jewish Museum in New York and the Anne Frank Museum in Amsterdam now have no value.

This editorial is published in a special issue of the *South Bulletin*[2] which focuses on the present crisis humanity faces in the holocaust now being perpetrated by the Jews of Israel on the people of Palestine. In his article in that issue, 'Holocaust Denied', John Pilger quotes the Soviet poet Yevtushenko: 'When the truth is replaced by silence,' the poet said, 'the silence is a lie.' Yevtushenko was asking why those who knew what was happening are silent. In relation to the war in Gaza, Pilger says, 'Among the Anglo-American intelligentsia ... (t)hey know that the horror now raining on Gaza has little to do with Hamas or, absurdly,

'Israel's right to exist.' They know the opposite to be true: that Palestine's right to exist was cancelled 61 years ago and the expulsion and, if necessary, extinction of the indigenous people was planned and executed by the founders of Israel.'

Also reproduced in that issue of the *South Bulletin* is what Mahatma Gandhi said on the subject in 1938 and 1946. 'My sympathies are all with the Jews,' he wrote, '...But my sympathy does not blind me to the requirements of justice. The cry for the national home for the Jews does not make much appeal to me. .... Why should they not, like other peoples of the earth, make that country their home where they are born and where they earn their livelihood?...If I were a Jew and were born in Germany,...I would claim Germany as my home even as the tallest gentile German may, and challenge him to shoot me or cast me in the dungeon; I would refuse to be expelled or to submit to discriminating treatment. And for doing this, I should not wait for the fellow Jews to join me in civil resistance but would have confidence that in the end the rest are bound to follow my example.'[3]

Gandhi goes on to say, 'Palestine belongs to the Arabs in the same sense that England belongs to the English or France to the French. It is wrong and inhuman to impose the Jews on the Arabs. What is going on in Palestine today cannot be justified by any moral code of conduct...Surely it would be a crime against humanity to reduce the proud Arabs so that Palestine can be restored to the Jews partly or wholly as their national home... And now a word to the Jews in Palestine...if they must look to the Palestine of geography as their national home, it is wrong to enter it under the shadow of the British gun...'[4]

Indeed, it was the British gun that created the state of Israel. In my own op-ed in the special issue, I show how the British violated the mandate on Palestine given to them by the League of Nations. On three occasions Britain promised the Arabs the setting up of a legislative body in Palestine and the cessation of Jewish immigration. All the promises were broken. Arab rebellions were ruthlessly crushed including, according to British records, the murder of 3,073 Arabs and punitive demolition of more than 2,000 houses through aerial bombardment. During the Second World War, nearly 30,000 Jewish men were trained by the British, and formed the core of the Haganah, later the Israel Defence Forces, which defeated the Arabs in 1948. It is clear that the British violated that trust. The General Assembly of the UN should set up a Commission of Inquiry to undertake the long-delayed evaluation of the British mandate in Palestine. *Did the British fulfil their mandate and their trust?*

The Jewish problem was always, historically, a European problem. In Shakespeare's *Merchant of Venice* (c.1599), the central and most despised character is the Jewish moneylender Shylock. Though Shylock is a tormented character, he is also a tormentor. In his *Othello, the Moor of Venice* (c. 1603), Othello, the black man, kills his wife, Desdemona, and yet Shakespeare presents him as a character that deserves sympathy and compassion. Throughout the centuries, a Jew in Europe was looked down upon more than a black man. It is with colonialism and the Jewish Holocaust in Europe that a reversal took place, with the black man despised and the Jews becoming an object of pity and guilt. To expiate their guilt Europe and America, instead of giving Jews their rights in their own countries, dumped them onto the colonised South.

Gandhi's advice to the Jews now holds good for the Arabs. They must fight for their rights where they are born, even if they are shot and cast into the dungeon, and even if Israel holds 12,000 of them prisoners in their dungeons. Israel, with all its military hardware and American technology designed to flush out the tunnels between Gaza and Egypt, will not defeat Hamas. Hamas is not just a few individuals. It is an idea, the idea of liberation from merciless exploitation and oppression. Israel cannot win. The fact is that the two-states solution primarily serves Euro-American broader interests in the Gulf area. The Euro-American alliance exploits the Jews in Israel, and in turn, Israel super-exploits and oppresses the Palestinians.

One casualty of the war in Gaza is the two-states solution. The question then is: What does the international community do with a *state* called Israel. There is a forgotten piece of history. When the British mandate over Palestine was created, the US Department of State, in supporting UN Resolution 181, had recommended the creation of separate Jewish and Arab *provinces*, not states. Now that the two-states solution has failed, the Palestinians should have their democratic right to create their one state, as should have happened if the British had been faithful to their mandate.

As for the Jews, I have a practical proposal. The only way the Americans and the Europeans can expiate their guilt over centuries of persecution of the Jews is to 'welcome them back home'. They can create, a province called Israel somewhere between Utah and California. It would cost US $ 2.5 million over a period of ten years. It can be done. 'We can do it', Obama!

Notes

1. See the *Independent* (2009) 9 January.
2. *South Bulletin: Reflections and Foresights* (2009) 16 January, www.southcentre.org.
3. Mohandas K. Gandhi (1938) 'A non-violent look at conflict & violence', *Harijan*, 26 November, http://www.kamat.com/mmgandhi/mideast.htm.
4. Gandhi (1938).

There is another way out of the present dilemma

16 January 2009

One casualty of the war in Gaza will be the two-state solution. The most bizarre irony of present history in the making is that as a direct result of Israeli war against the population of Gaza the present proposed 'solution' to the Palestine–Israel question based on the theory of two states has now suffered a possibly fatal blow.

The Israel–Palestine situation is a classic case of a historical predicament, a situation from which extrication appears almost impossible. There are many intractable conflict situations in the world, but the Israel–Palestine problem is almost unique – a global (rather than regional) problem as we shall explain below. It has reached a point where the two populations are set on a course of mutual destruction. It is a problem that has festered for over 60 years in our own times and for centuries before. The balance of military forces favour Israel for the time being and what appears as an attempt on its part to destroy the Palestinians. But the situation could reverse itself in another generation, and with the memory of Gaza in the background, the Arabs might seek the total destruction of Jews – at least in Israel. Israel will not succeed in the total destruction of Hamas, or the ideology of Hamas, or the forced removal of the Palestinians from their present lands to Jordan or Egypt or other Arab countries. So then the question is: If the Palestinians cannot be removed from Palestine, are there other solutions that might be considered?

The reasons why a two-state solution is now not going to work can be grouped under three main headings:

1. Increasing recognition that the two-state solution is a fraud: it is part of US–EU global geopolitical and energy–security strategy presented as a 'Palestine problem'
2. Increasing questioning of the legitimacy of the creation of Israel in 1947
3. Increasing recognition by Palestinians that the future is ultimately on their side, and they can afford to wait.

The two-state solution

In the early days following the 27 December 2008 attack on Gaza some commentators tried to portray it as an election strategy to help the rival parties in Israel win votes. However, it turns out that it is a deeper issue. In our view this, for Israel, is its last war for survival. Israel feels threatened by the presence of Hamas in Gaza, and is now carrying out a massive assault on the leadership of Hamas and the people of Gaza in order to effect a 'final solution' (to use an analogy from Jewish history) to what they see as threatening their very survival as a state.

For the West, it is a war for the protection of their vital geopolitical interests in the Middle East, especially access to oil and maritime routes and air space. There is a common perception that Israel is the driving force behind events in the Middle East. Up to a point this is true. The most visible part of the war is the barrage of air attacks and Israeli tanks marching into high-density areas of Gaza. But this is only part of the truth and probably a smaller part. The larger part of the truth is that Israel is being used by the United States and Europe for their own wider geopolitical and energy–security reasons. Of course, admittedly, Israel and the US–EU alliance use each other – Israel to secure its survival as a state, and the US–EU to advance and protect their geopolitical-energy interests.

There is, however, one significant difference. For the Jews in Israel, there are other ways in which they can escape from the mayhem in the Middle East (go to Europe, for example), or for the entire Jewish nation to protect their lives and lifestyles outside the geographical confines of the land presently known as 'Israel' (a point to which I shall come later). For the US and Europe, on the other hand, to safeguard their geopolitical and energy interests, they need the state of Israel to be firmly located within the geographic space of the Middle East and the Gulf area. In other words, in the present situation, the US–EU alliance needs Israel more than the other way around. I am aware that this is contrary to public perception of the matter. This public perception, however, is seriously flawed. *The fact is that the Americans and the Europeans exploit the Jews in Israel, and in turn, Israel super-exploits and oppresses the Palestinians.*

To understand these complex and inter-connected issues, which provide the context of the war in Gaza, one needs to take a long view of history and from a broad landscape. Because, in our view, Israel is primarily a bridgehead of the West in the strategic region of the Middle East and the Persian Gulf, it is necessary to begin with the present crisis in the West and then analyse how the war in Gaza is symptomatic of the larger Western crisis. Israel is part of the West, and it has its problems. However, it can solve some of these problems without the West. The West, on the other hand, cannot protect its interests without the security of Israel. Thus, when the US and the European Union advocate a two-state solution to the 'problem of Palestine' (which itself is a biased and racist definition of the problem), they are, in actual fact, only serving their own interests. For them to pretend that they are mediators and honest brokers in the conflict between Israel and Palestine is a mockery of both history and present reality. The two-state solution has always been a fraud, as the analysis below will show.

Consider first the changes in the global geopolitics of the last 30 years and in the last five years. From about 1975 to 2007 was a period, first, of intensified cold war (up to about 1989), then its end with the collapse of the Soviet Union and the emergence of the United States as a single hegemon (from 1989 to about 2001), and then during the last five or six years the rise of the South and the relative decline of the North as we enter into the next 25- or 30-year generational cycle.

The period 1975 to 2007 started with deepening multiple crises in the West. Among these were:

- The geopolitical and security crisis following the loss of colonies in the preceding 25 years
- The oil crises of 1975 and 1979
- The entry of the Soviet Union into Afghanistan
- The Islamic revolution in Iran in 1979, which changed the entire political scene from the Caspian Sea to Palestine, making the West extremely insecure
- Internally, the West faced a deepening crisis of profitability and increasing pressure from the working classes.

However, by 1989 the West emerged from these crises triumphant, not only domestically but also internationally. With the initiatives taken by Margaret Thatcher and Ronald Reagan under deregulation and market liberalisation, the ruling classes and corporate capital were able first to discipline the working classes within their own countries and then inaugurate a whole series of policy measures domestically and internationally, which later came to be identified as 'neoliberal globalisation' based on the so-called Washington Consensus. These measures boiled down essentially to trade and market liberalisation; privatisation and deregulation; and the promotion of the private sector.

That period has effectively ended. The financial meltdown in the West is not a mere trade cyclical phenomenon. Experts now agree that the West has not seen a worse crisis since the Great Depression of the 1930s. In 1930 the US Congress passed the Smoot-Hatley Tariff Act triggering the Great Depression by creating trade barriers. Today, even those corporations such as Lehmann Brothers and Goldman Sachs that survived the 1930s have collapsed like a house of cards. The state take-over of banks and other productive assets of the private sector has demonstrated, finally, that the private sector is not 'the engine of growth' as the neoliberal ideology would have us believe. It is a state-subsidised, exploitative, greedy and self-indulgent sector. In other words, there is an ideological collapse of the system.

At the political–military level, the US-dominated unicentric world is now replaced by a polycentric world. The virtual defeat of the US in Afghanistan and Iraq – wars that have lasted longer than the Second World War – has shaken American belief in its infallibility, and diminished the South's awe for the US or for its 'coalition of the willing'. The US no longer enjoys the strategic, tactical or moral high ground that it had just 10 or 15 years ago. However, losing credibility and legitimacy does not mean the US will become less aggressive. Indeed, as its moral authority declines, the US could become even more aggressive militarily. It could intervene directly or it could use proxies like Israel, which is exactly what is happening today in Gaza.

In terms of access to global resources, the US is facing serious challenges regionally, in its own backyard, and globally. The prices of oil, minerals and metals showed a steady climb from

2001 to 2006, and then from 2007 on they were on a roller coaster, with prices swinging bizarrely up and down, with uncertain futures markets. This is compounded by new assertive popular movements in the countries of the South for claiming ownership of land, oil, minerals and other natural resources. The Venezuelan boldness in nationalising oil is inspiring others to follow suit. In May 2006, Bolivia's President Evo Morales signed a decree placing his country's energy industry under state control. In April 2007, US lawyers representing 24 indigenous Peruvians sued Occidental Petroleum, the California-based company that made a fortune from the Peruvian rain forest from 1972 to 2000. In a Los Angeles court, the lawyers alleged that, among other offences, by dumping toxic wastewater directly into rivers and streams, the company was endangering the lives and health of people. For indigenous peoples, the action by Peruvian Indians is emblematic of a new era. In February 2008, President Hugo Chavez threatened to cut off oil sales to the United States if ExxonMobil pursues international court orders it has obtained against billions of dollars of Venezuelan state assets in a contract dispute.

In Africa, oil has become a security and military issue for America. Its Africa Command (AFRICOM), with an increased military presence on the continent, has targeted seven countries in the oil-rich region of the Gulf of Guinea (Cameroon, Equatorial Guinea, Gabon, Ghana, Liberia, São Tomé and Príncipe, and Senegal).

These are difficult times for the US and the EU; it is a different world. Some of the predictions made about the future by American experts make interesting reading. For example, in its publicly accessible document *Global Trends 2025*, the US National Intelligence Council draws out alternative futures for US policy consideration based on seven variables: the Globalising Economy; Demographics of Discord; the New Players; Scarcity in the Midst of Plenty; Growing Potential for Conflict; Challenges of the International System; and the US in a Power-sharing World. Among some of its 'predictions' relevant to this essay are the following:[1]

- 'By 2025 a single "international community" composed of nation-states will no longer exist. Power will be more dispersed with the newer players bringing new rules of the game while risks will increase that the traditional Western alliances will weaken.'

- 'Shrinking economic and military capabilities may force the US into a difficult set of tradeoffs between domestic versus foreign policy priorities.'
- 'All current technologies are inadequate for replacing traditional energy architecture on the scale needed.' Iran and Russia will increase power unless non-fossil transition is made by 2025. 'With high oil and gas prices, major exporters such as Russia and Iran will substantially augment their levels of national power, with Russia's GDP potentially approaching that of the UK and France.'
- 'The potential for conflict will increase owing to rapid changes in parts of the greater Middle East and the spread of lethal capabilities.'
- 'Episodes of low-intensity conflict and terrorism taking place under a nuclear umbrella could lead to an unintended escalation and broader conflict.'

Like the US, Europe too is facing a difficult future. The European Union is very conscious of the competition from the so-called emerging economies of Brazil, China, India, Russia and South Africa. It risks loss of markets in the South, especially in its former colonies in Africa and semi-colonies in Asia and Latin America. The reliability of access to oil and raw materials at affordable prices has seriously challenged European diplomacy (for example, in the present dispute between Russia and Ukraine) and it has increased the urgency to look for alternative sources of fuel and energy. The battle lines of the future are already being drawn in terms of access to and exploitation of oil wells, minerals and natural resources.

The EU has a vigorous and aggressive 'Global Europe' strategy. The Lisbon strategy sets out a coherent agenda for adapting European economies to the new global environment, and preparing its corporations and citizens for a 'Citizen's Agenda' that examines how the internal European market can further help European business make the changes necessary to compete internationally 'by diversifying, specialising and innovating'.[2] More than ever, the EU needs to import to export. In 2006 the European Commission issued an 'Action Plan for EU External Competitiveness', which, among other things, said: 'The Commission will bring forward a communication on a renewed Market Access Strategy in early 2007. This is likely to involve setting regular priorities in terms of sectors and markets where the removal of trade barriers would create the greatest gains for EU exporters. The Commission will need to concentrate resources in key countries, invest in technical expertise, co-ordinate policy tools and work more closely with Member States and industry/exporters.'

The OECD strategy, led by Europe, of tying Africa to its aid apron strings through the Paris Declaration on Aid Effectiveness is part of the overall European strategy to ensure access to markets, oil and natural resources.[3]

Against the background of these disturbing trends for the US and the EU, they now need Israel more than ever. There is, however, a history of close collaboration between North America, Europe and Israel. The Bush administration has long pushed the 'laptop documents' – 1,000 pages of technical documents supposedly stolen by Israel intelligence from an Iranian laptop – as 'hard evidence' of Iranian intentions to develop nuclear weapons. Between Britain and Israel there is close collaboration on how to counter terrorism – 'Operation Kratos' is the code word used by the Anti-Terrorist Branch (SO13) of London's Metropolitan Police Service to refer to policies surrounding and including 'shoot-to-kill' tactics to be used in dealing with suspected terrorists and suicide bombers. The tactics are understood to be based, in part, on consultation with Israeli and Sri Lankan law enforcement agencies on how to deal with 'deadly and determined' attackers. The Canada–Israel Public Security Agreement is a collaborative project to counter terrorism. The Israel–NATO Framework Agreement on Military Build-up in the Eastern Mediterranean and the Persian Gulf is directed against Iran, Syria and Lebanon. It is also related to the deployment of US naval forces in the Persian Gulf.

All three – North America, Europe and Israel – share the same political, ideological and strategic terrain. To pretend that the UK and the US – or their government allies in the Arab states (guess who?) – can be honest brokers between Israel and Palestine is simply ridiculous. They all fear Iran's rise to power, and the increased power of the resistance movements in Iraq, Palestine and Lebanon. There are soft power theorists in these countries that argue that a hard militarist line with Iran or Palestine could backfire. But it would appear that the distinction between hard power and soft power is relative, a point that President Obama will soon demonstrate. Obama, after all, is answerable to his electorate, and to his own Congress. On 11 January 2009 the Congress voted to support Israeli action in Gaza by a vote of 390 to 5. The next day, the United Nations Human Rights Council, by a vote of 33 to 1 with 13 abstentions 'strongly condemned the ongoing Israeli military operation which had resulted in massive violations of human rights of the Palestinian people and systematic destruction of the Palestinian infrastructure.'[4]

Within President Obama's close cabinet there is Vice-President Joe Biden, who was hawkish on Iraq and a known Zionist; chief of staff Rahm Emanuel, who is a hard-line supporter of Israel's 'targeted assassination' policy and actually volunteered to work with the Israeli army during the 1991 Gulf War; Susan Rice, an Iraq hawk who promoted the myth that Saddam Hussein had weapons of mass destruction, and who advocated the bombing of Sudan; and above all, there is Hillary Clinton who defended the Iraq war, backed the bombing of Yugoslavia, and favours bombing Iran. The US supplied Israel with 250-pound 'smart' GBU-39 bombs on the eve of the attack on Gaza. The president-elect could not have not known about this; indeed, it is hardly likely that the action would have been taken without his knowledge.

So why are the Americans and the Europeans working hand-in-glove with Israel? What is at stake? At stake, besides the strategic interests mentioned earlier, is the control and ownership of strategic offshore gas reserves off the Gaza coastline. The rights to the offshore gas field are held 90 per cent by British Gas (BG) and its Athens based partner Consolidated Contractors (CCC), owned by some rich Lebanese families; the remaining 10 per cent is held by the Investment Fund of the Palestinian Authority (PA).[5] The CCC has a 25-year agreement for oil and gas exploration rights signed in November 1999 with the PA. The BG–CCC–PA agreement includes field development and the construction of a gas pipeline.[6] The licence covers the entire offshore marine area of Gaza, which is contiguous to several Israeli offshore gas facilities. BG estimates Gaza reserves to be around 1.4 trillion cubic feet, valued at approximately $4 billion. In 2006, BG 'was close to signing a deal to pump the gas to Egypt.'[7] Under the proposed

2007 agreement with BG, Palestinian gas from Gaza's offshore wells was to be channelled by an undersea pipeline to the Israeli seaport of Ashkelon, thereby transferring control over the sale of the natural gas to Israel. These various offshore installations are also linked up to Israel's energy transport corridor, extending from the port of Eilat, which is an oil pipeline terminal, on the Red Sea to the seaport-pipeline terminal at Ashkelon, and northwards to Haifa, and eventually linking up through a proposed Israeli–Turkish pipeline with the Turkish port of Ceyhan. Ceyhan is the terminal of the Baku, Tblisi Ceyhan Trans Caspian pipeline. What is envisaged is to link the BTC pipeline to the Trans-Israel Eilat-Ashkelon pipeline, also known as Israel's Tipline.[8]

As can be seen, it is a complex picture of interconnected interests that link a major British oil corporation, Israel, Egypt, Turkey, some rich families in the Lebanon and, above all, Fatah and the Palestine Authority under the control of Mahmoud Abbas. Here is where, to the consternation of the above coalition of forces, Hamas put a fly in the ointment. As long as Gaza was under Fatah's control, the Western coalition felt relatively secure. The electoral victory of Hamas in Gaza, however, has raised the spectre of billions of dollars going into the coffers of a 'terrorist' group. Sooner or later, it was clear to all these parties (and not just Israel) that Gaza had to be invaded and Hamas removed from power. According to Israeli military sources, the invasion plan for the Gaza Strip under 'Operation Cast Lead' was set in motion in June 2008.[9] At the same time, Israel contacted British Gas with a view to resuming suspended negotiations for the purchase of Gaza's natural gas. Israel was already setting in motion a new dispensation on the assumption that Hamas would be quickly wiped out in a military blitzkrieg.

This explains why the US and the EU have declared Hamas a 'terrorist organisation', and why they (and Egypt and Turkey) are now emerging as 'mediators' and 'honest brokers', while still pursuing the two-state solution. Egypt and Fatah did not attend the 16 January 2009 Arab summit in Qatar. The summit strongly supported Hamas and the Palestinian resistance.

The legitimacy of the creation of Israel

The Arabs of Palestine have never accepted the creation of the Jewish state. What was victory for the Jews was regarded by the Arabs as the Nakba, meaning the catastrophe. Indeed it was not until 1988, 40 years after Israel's birth, that Yasser Arafat's Palestine Liberation Organisation (PLO) renounced its goal of liberating the whole of Palestine. And it took another five years before it agreed to the Oslo Peace Accords, which most Palestinians now regard as a grave error on the part of PLO. The Oslo Accords gave no firm promise of a Palestinian state in return for the recognition of Israel. In fact, most Palestinians equate what was created with Norwegian mediation as comparable to the state of South Africa under the apartheid rule – 'fragmented Bantustans'. As Fatah became more and more dependent on Western aid, the newly installed Palestinian Authority grew more corrupt, and more and more Palestinians turned to Hamas. Hamas, born in 1987 as an offshoot of Egypt's Muslim Brotherhood, built its credibility through social programmes, a reputation for honesty, and a refusal to capitulate to the Oslo Accords and to the two-state solution.

Now the very circumstances under which Israel was created are coming under closer scrutiny. At the time of the UN partition resolution, the Jews of Palestine numbered only 600,000, mostly from Europe, and the Arabs more than twice that number. In the war that ensued, more than 600,000 of Palestine's Arabs were put to flight. Now, in the aftermath of the humanitarian carnage in Gaza, more and more people (and not just the Palestinians) would want to question the legitimacy of the process in the UN that led to the partition of Palestine and the creation of the state of Israel.

The Jewish problem was always historically a European problem, not a Palestinian problem. During the 19th century the spread of the Enlightenment across Europe led to the emancipation of Jews. But it also led to reaction against them. Jews were seen as alien and were not granted citizenship, for example. The growth of nationalism in Europe also created anti-Semitism and pogroms against the Jews, culminating in the brutal Holocaust under the Nazis, when 6 million European Jews perished.

After the First World War Britain was granted a mandate over Palestine by the League of Nations. In a duplicitous manner, Britain denied the people of Palestine their democratic rights, surreptitiously encouraged the Jews to enter Palestine, while preserving good relations with the Arabs to protect their oil and other strategic interests. 'On at least three occasions in thirty years,' Arthur Koestler, the famous Jewish–Hungarian–British author, wrote in *Promise and Fulfilment* (1949), 'the Arabs had been promised the setting up of a legislative body, the cessation of Jewish immigration and a check on Jewish economic expansion.'[10] And on each of these occasions, Britain broke its promise. Rebellions against the British were ruthlessly suppressed. According to British records, the administration killed 3,073 Arabs (112 of whom were executed). These figures exclude Arabs killed by Zionist organisations or the Jewish Special Night Squads under the command of British intelligence officers. During the uprisings, British security forces used the standard tactics of anti-colonial warfare – torture, murder, collective punishment, detention without trial, military courts, aerial bombardment and punitive demolition of more than 2,000 houses (like what is happening in Gaza today). During the Second World War, nearly 30,000 Jewish men of the Yishuv volunteered for the British army. These soldiers would become the core of the Haganah, later the Israel Defence Forces, which defeated the Arabs in 1948.

However, when the vote was taken in the General Assembly of the UN on 29 November 1947 for the creation of the state of Israel, Britain abstained. In any case, it did not matter. The geopolitical configuration at the time favoured the US and the Europeans. Here was an opportunity for them to 'solve' the problem of the Jews by dumping them in the Middle East. It is worth recalling who voted how. The 33 countries that cast a 'Yes' vote were: Australia, Belgium, Bolivia, Brazil, Byelorussia, Canada, Costa Rica, Czechoslovakia, Denmark, Dominican Republic, Ecuador, France, Guatemala, Haiti, Iceland, Liberia, Luxembourg, Netherlands, New Zealand, Nicaragua, Norway, Panama, Paraguay, Peru, Philippines, Poland, Sweden, Ukraine, South Africa (then under apartheid), USSR, USA, Uruguay, and Venezuela. The 13 countries that voted 'No' were: Afghanistan, Cuba, Egypt, Greece, India, Iran, Iraq, Lebanon, Pakistan, Saudi Arabia, Syria, Turkey and Yemen. The 10 countries that abstained were: Argentina, Chile, China, Colombia, El Salvador, Ethiopia,

Honduras, Mexico, United Kingdom and Yugoslavia. Switching their votes between 25 November and 29 November, to provide the necessary two-thirds majority, were Liberia, the Philippines and Haiti, all heavily dependent on the United States.[11] On 10 November 1945, US diplomats from the Mid-East had tried to persuade President Truman not to yield to Zionist pressure. He replied: 'I'm sorry, gentlemen, but I have to answer to hundreds of thousands who are anxious for the success of Zionism: I do not have hundreds of thousands of Arabs among my constituents.'[12]

It is important to note that had the UN been more universal in its membership in 1947, and had countries from the South been able to vote without pressure from the US and Europe, Israel would have had no chance to secure a majority vote, let alone a two-thirds vote; there would have been no state of Israel. Today, however, the problem is described as a 'security' issue and taken to the Security Council of the UN where the West has three vetoes – those of the US, UK and France. The General Assembly has been emasculated of the power it had in 1947. Nonetheless, it is symptomatic of the new situation that the president of the General Assembly, Father Miguel d'Escoto Brockmann, has condemned Israeli action as 'genocide'.[13]

History is ultimately on their side

The third factor that spells doom for the two-state solution is the increasing recognition by Palestinians that history and the future is ultimately on their side. The global geopolitical situation has changed radically in favour of the Palestinians.

As Benny Morris, professor of Middle Eastern history at Ben-Gurion University, says, public opinion in the West is gradually losing support for Israel and the holocaust is now 'a faint and ineffectual memory'.[14] He says 'the walls are closing in' over Israel in the form of Iran's nuclear threat, the rise of Hamas and Arab anger.

Even in the United States young American Jews today do not care about Israel. A 2007 study, which polled 1,700 American Jews, found American Jewish detachment from Israel is growing and strongest among younger Jews. The study, conducted by Professors Steven M. Cohen and Ari Y. Kelman, found that of

American Jews under 35, less than half (48 per cent) felt 'Israel's destruction would be a personal tragedy' and slightly over half (54 percent) were 'comfortable with the idea of a Jewish State.'[15]

An increasing number of Jewish intellectuals and human rights activists – among them Yuri Avnery, Tom Segev, Ilan Pappe, Gideon Levy, Amira Hass, Noam Chomsky, Dennis Kucinich, Norman Finkelstein and Richard Falk – publicly condemn Israeli crimes. Richard Falk, the UN special rapporteur for human rights in the occupied territories and a renowned professor of international law at Princeton, was refused entry into Israel in December last year, detained for 20 hours and deported. Falk says that Israeli treatment of Palestinians is no different from the Nazi record of collective atrocity.

In Palestine, the balance of political forces is shifting ineluctably towards Hamas. As Jewish settlement in the West Bank has accelerated, as the Palestine Authority, under the weight of 'aid' from the West, has grown more corrupt, and as negotiations with Israel make no progress, people have turned to Hamas. Hamas, by contrast, is very practical and very effective and steadfast in its resolution not to endorse a permanent peace based on the Western-driven two-state solution. Israel (with the complicity of the West and probably of some Arab states) is bombing and strafing Gaza (still going after over three weeks at the time of writing) in the hope of either eliminating the Hamas leadership or getting the people to rise up against Hamas, or both. Israel has failed, to the obvious frustration of its Western and Arab allies.

There is rising tension between the Arab streets as opposed to the Arab states. Popular anger at what they see as complicity on the part of some Arab states is mounting. As for the 1.1 million Arabs in Israel, their situation is worse than that of the black population in South Africa during its worst days under apartheid. The Israel-based Arabs are increasingly isolated from their brethren. Israel bars them, as its citizens, from travelling to Gaza and to most Arab countries. Their cousins in the occupied territories are unable to visit them. These are potential resistance fighters even if the present Hamas is emasculated.[16]

'Hamas will win the war, no matter what happens,' Yuri Avnery, once an Israeli soldier and now a peace activist, said. 'They will be considered by hundreds of millions of Arabs heroes who have recovered the dignity and pride of Arab nations. If at the end of the war they are still standing in Gaza this will be a huge victory for them, to hold out against this huge Israeli army and firepower will be an incredible achievement. They will gain even more than Hezbollah did during the last war.' [17]

As the British journal, *The Economist*, in its editorial on 10 January 2006, said, 'But even in the event of Israel "winning" in Gaza, a hundred years of war suggest that the Palestinians cannot be silenced by brute force. Hamas will survive, and with it that strain in Arab thinking which says that a Jewish state does not belong in the Middle East.' It went on: 'The most promising moment of all came at the beginning of this decade, with Mr Clinton's near-miss at Camp David. But now, with the rise of Hamas and the war in Gaza, the brief period of relative hope is in danger of flickering out.' [18]

That, then, raises the question: If the idea of two states is 'flickering out', and if the Arab thinking that 'a Jewish state does not belong in the Middle East' gains strength, as undoubtedly it would, what then is to happen to the Jews of Israel? Is there an alternative solution to the two-state solution?

An alternative proposal

The problem is that nobody has seriously applied his or her mind to this question. The idea of the two states has become an embedded reality in the mind of most people for so long that any alternative thinking has literally been foreclosed as a possibility. This false illusion of two states as reality has been stubbornly sustained by the Western and Israeli propaganda machines, backed by billions of dollars of American annual subsidy to the state of Israel and a formidable war machine that everybody assumed would always win wars against the Palestinians.

This has not happened. The West has succeeded in co-opting a number of Arab and Moslem states (and Fatah) to the two-state solution imposed on the people of Palestine in 1947. It is now 61 years later, but the two peoples – Jews and the Palestinians – have proven incapable of finding an acceptable formula that both sides can live with. Israel has always pushed for the two-state idea on its terms, and to get its way it has regularly and systematically resorted to forced occupation and violence verging on genocide. Fatah might have accepted a compromise after the Oslo Accords, but Hamas has taken a firm line of resistance, the Arab streets have come out to challenge the Arab states, and now with the carnage of Gaza, the possibility of compromise is virtually ruled out. At Camp David in 2000 with all the diplomatic charm offensive of President Clinton, and almost servile docility of Abbas, an agreement evaded them. The UN resolution had partitioned Jerusalem, but it was not possible, because of Israeli stubbornness, to agree on how to implement it. There are now double the numbers of Palestinian refugees. They still demand to go back to their homeland. Israeli settlers have been occupying more and more of their lands and have attacked even their refugee settlements. Israel has now experienced that the land it vacates such as Gaza, even under siege, could become a bridgehead for Hamas and for resistance.

If anybody still harbours the illusion of the two states, then they are refusing to face reality, or have such powerful vested interests in the two-state idea that an alternative is hard to contemplate. Both history and current events show that Israel is an artificial implant on the land and body politic of Palestine to serve US–EU global strategic interests, and to 'dump' what was historically a problem created by European racism on to the land of the Palestinians.

However bizarre it may sound, the paradox of history is that the bigger obstacle to looking for an alternative solution might not be the Jewish people but the United States and Europe. Why? Because it is the US and Europe that need Israel implanted in Palestine and the Gulf area for the protection of their global strategic interests, now even more than ever before. The Jews' emotional attachment to the state of Israel is as powerful today as was, for example, the white settler population of South Africa 10–15 years ago. But odd as it may sound today, if a more peaceful environment was offered to the ordinary citizens of Israel, where they could engage in life's daily routines, go for prayers, enjoy the swimming pool, dance in the clubs, and enjoy sports, they could adjust to a new reality sooner than most people imagine.

When matters came to a head, the white population of South Africa had to adjust to a new reality. For nearly 300 years (five times longer than the 'state' of Israel) they had thought of themselves as a distinct Boer nation. But when finally faced with the reality of resistance by the African masses, many of the whites had a change of conscience, and became activists in bringing about the new dispensation. Most settled down in the new state; those who could not adjust, emigrated.

When reality catches up and opens up locked-up minds in Israel, and a brighter future is offered to the Jews of Israel (say a parcel of land in the United States), they might exercise the options of either emigrating or adjusting to the new reality of one state – the state of Palestine, with an Arab majority and a substantial Jewish minority. If nothing else, the demographic reality will catch up. A recent issue of *Time* magazine[19] says that 'A higher growth rate means that Arabs in Israel and the territories will soon vastly outnumber Jews there.' It estimates the Jewish population will rise from 5.4 million at present to 6.4 million in 2020. The corresponding figures for Arabs are 5.5 million and 8.5 million. But demographics apart, it is the politics that have changed. Hamas is not just a bunch of individuals. It is a powerful idea, the idea of resistance even at the cost of dear lives. That idea is now likely to outlive all the violence Israel can inflict on the millions of refugees living on its borders who cherish the will 'to go back home'.

So between the two present strong protagonists of the two-state solution – the US–EU alliance (backed for convenience by a few Arab states and Fatah) and the state of Israel (with a population yearning for peace) – it is the AU–EU alliance (that ironically, and one might say tragicomically, offers itself as mediators and honest brokers) that is the bigger obstacle. In this paper we do not address the issue of what the US and Europe would do in the absence of Israel to fight their strategic battles for them in the Gulf area and the Middle East. This will evolve as part of the movement of history itself, just as the former Soviet Union (now Russia) had to adjust to the reality of the collapse of the Soviet Union and the absorption of its former allies or satellites into Western Europe.

Where now?

Nobody should underestimate the complexity and seeming intractability of the problem. Nonetheless, it is in times such as this (for South Africa it was their military defeat in Quito-Carnavale in Angola that was the turning point) that wiser and far-thinking leaders from all sides (governments, civil society, churches, the United Nations) must put in motion processes that can open doors to the future, however difficult it may be to envisage it today. We offer one possible route towards forward thinking. The language of death and destruction (bordering on genocide) is definitely not an option. The obvious point to start with is the question: If the two communities – Jews and Palestinians – cannot live with one another, what do we do?

Israel has been trying to push the Palestinians to migrate to Jordan, Egypt and Lebanon (if possible) and other Arab lands. But this is not going to happen. First, these countries are themselves so crowded and politically so vulnerable that an influx of Palestinians could alter their delicate balance of forces, which would ironically spell disaster even for Israel. Consider 'Gazas' multiplying in Jordan, Lebanon, Syria, etc. Second, in any case, the Palestinians have set their minds to returning to the homelands, a vision that Hamas has inspired. That vision will not disappear. Hamas has offered a 30-year truce to Israel without recognising it. Why? Because Hamas knows (and Israel too) that in 30 years (another generation), the demographics will have changed and more to the point the politics would have changed.

Could the Palestinians be removed physically to some place outside the Middle East – say in Europe or America? Can they be offered secure homes, jobs, and peace outside the present mayhem? In terms of the availability of land (especially in America or Canada), or availability of finance (say about US$ 2.5 billion over a period of ten years) it is not something that can be dismissed out of hand. Alternatively, can the same be offered to the Jews of Israel – land and peace outside of the Middle East?

Between the two – Jews or Palestinians – who might be more willing to move, and to be acceptable to the receiving countries? Based on my knowledge of history and some understanding of cultures and climes, I would venture to hedge the bet that the prospect for the Jews to move might appear to be a more feasible proposition than that of the Palestinians. After all, the Jewish question was a major political issue in Europe in the 19th century; it became worse in the 20th century with the Holocaust. The creation of Israel (at a time when most countries of the South were still under colonial or semi-colonial rule) was an attempt to resolve the centuries old European problem by dumping it on to the Middle East. But in doing so, the US and Europe only succeeded in compounding the problem, and universalising it. Arguably, much of Islamic anger (especially of the youth) that feeds Islamic fundamentalism and extremism (in the countries of the South but also in those of the North) owes itself to this egregious injustice done to the people of Palestine.

Would the Jews want to move? Maybe not immediately. Maybe not all of them. Most of them still believe, or are made to believe, that the land of Palestine was a gift of God to 'the chosen people'. This myth (for that is what it is) is difficult to kill, and will take time to die. After all, there are hundreds of such myths which communities all over the world (not just Jews) entertain in their dreams. Just try Africa or the Pacific Islands for a start. Besides, if the Jews claim Palestine as their 'ancestral land', by the holy dispensation of their gods, why should that dispensation be binding on the gods of other communities, religions or cultures? This is not to dismiss the Jews' legitimate claim to visit and pray at their holy shrines in the Middle East. But to exaggerate these claims into embedding a whole state in the midst of an alien culture, and creating death and destruction in its wake, can hardly be history's wisdom. The Americans and Europeans have tried it, but the experiment has failed, and we must now move on.

The real possibility that the Jews may be persuaded to move is also supported by Jewish history itself. At the Sixth Zionist Congress at Basel on 26 August 1903, Herzl, the father of the Jewish nation, proposed settlement in Uganda (my country). The British, imperial masters of Uganda, accepted the proposal. Fortunately for my country, the plan was finally abandoned, for had it been implemented, we would today have the same mayhem in Eastern and Southern Africa that we have in Palestine and the Middle East.

Many Jews may not move out of present Israel but many might – maybe even a quarter of the present population – if the prospect of a future is brighter than what Israel has to offer them. The religious and cultural affiliations of Israeli Jews vary widely: 55 per cent say they are 'traditional'; 20 per cent consider themselves to be 'secular Jews'; 17 per cent define themselves as 'Orthodox Jews'; and the final 8 per cent define themselves as 'Haredi Jews'. Because of this plurality and a democratic culture, the political system allows for proportional representation. But this means none of the three major parties has a chance of gaining power by itself. This creates an almost chaotic political culture, where intricate bargaining between parties and groups within parties can sustain or destroy 'coalitions' in power. Israel may pride itself on being a 'democratic' state, but so did South Africa under apartheid. What kind of democracy is this? It is far more sensible for the democratic-minded Jews of Israel to find another location in the world where they would be able to practise real democracy – and also the wonderful socialist idea of the kibbutz – in peace, harmony and justice.

Which of the populations of present Israel could move, if properly inspired and motivated, and where? If the location is attractive enough, many of the traditional, Orthodox and Haredi Jews could consider moving, let us say to land near Utah or Nevada in the USA. Or it may be a generational matter: many younger people might consider moving where the older ones might not want to.

This is just an example, but let us explore it further. Some 150 years ago, many members of the Church of Jesus Christ of Latter-Day Saints (LDS) moved to the US. One sect of the LDS constitutes the Mormons. Led by Brigham Young and his group of pioneers they settled in Utah near Salt Lake City. Mormonism has close historical affinity to Judaism. It has incorporated many Old Testament ideas into its theology, and it has many cultural similarities. Among the early Mormon settlements, the largest was called Nauvoo, which in Hebrew means 'to be beautiful'. Brigham Young named a tributary of the Great Salt Lake the 'Jordan River'. The LDS Church created a writing called the 'Deseret Alphabet', which was based, in part, on Hebrew. The LDS Church has a Jerusalem Centre in Israel, where young people learn to appreciate and respect the region. Not surprisingly, Utah also has places called South Jordan and West Jordan, and Zion National Park.

This could be a place worth considering by the Jews of Israel – not necessarily within the midst of the Mormons. However, there are still vast tracts of unoccupied lands in Utah and Nevada to which traditional, Orthodox or Haredi Jews from Israel might contemplate moving. From there the beaches of California are not far – a single day's car journey to a more peaceful environment than along the Mediterranean Sea. They should, of course, have a right to visit Jerusalem and other holy shrines in the Middle East and they could come as tourists for an occasional nostalgic dip in the Mediterranean. They must not lose everything in moving out of Israel.

How much would this transmigration cost, over what period, and where would the funds come from? Before this process of calculation begins, the US and European nations have to go through the transformative process of a vision or mind shift. They have to recognise that they have failed to universalise their guilt over the holocaust, and indeed the opposite is what is happening – Israel itself is turning from victim to perpetrator of crimes against humanity. They have to acknowledge that while Israel is fast losing sympathy in the world, the Palestinians led by the Hamas movement (for that is what it is) is fast gaining sympathy. The US and Europe need also to realise that much of the 'terrorist' and 'non-terrorist' anger comes from the obvious sense of injustice that Arab streets and Moslem masses feel about the situation in Palestine.

In South Africa, Western countries, having supported the racist regime for decades, had to face the changed reality. The time has come to recognise the coming reality on the ground in Palestine too. The West would have to acknowledge that a one-state solution is the only way forward.[20] The best option for the West would be to reduce their dependence on oil from the Middle East (which, in any case, the present US administration realises is its only sustainable option), make peace with the Arab nations and Iran, and lift the burden from Israel to look after their geo-strategic interests in the Gulf area. In other words, the West should re-align their strategic interests and alliances. They should then work towards a single, secular state in Palestine, with an Arab majority and a substantial Jewish minority with democratic rights.

Once a visionary leadership in the West realises this and takes the initiative, it should not be too difficult for Israel to produce a de Klerk kind of visionary realist within Israel, and for Palestine to produce a Mandela among the Arabs. They are probably there already, but they are not given an opportunity to shine. The Jewish leadership should be offered an opportunity to send an advance party to the US to identify lands where a willing population from among the Israeli Jews might be prepared to move over, say, the next ten years.

The financial question, then, becomes a less onerous challenge. The US presently provides about $2.5 billion a year in subsidy to the state of Israel. The US should negotiate with the European Union, the Arab nations, and the rich Jewish population in the US and Europe to put equivalent amounts of $2.5 billion a year each into a translocation fund. An annual amount of $10 billion would still be a small fraction of what they presently spend on armaments and 'anti-terrorist' activities, and a fraction of what they are presently spending on baling out the banks. This is not such a large amount for bringing peace and justice to an area which has festered in war and violence for over 50 years, costing trillions of dollars, the lives of thousands, incarceration and torture of tens of thousands, and which has been a major factor fanning Arab hostility and 'terrorist' activities.

If every young Jewish couple in Israel were offered compensation and translocation costs to voluntarily translocate outside of Israel, $10 billion would help settle some 100,000 couples a year with a compensation package of $100,000 each. Over the first ten years, half a million people might opt to move, if given an opportunity. The important point is not the numbers, but the principle behind it. Not many minorities in the world have that opportunity. Most poor people in Africa, Asia and Latin America who wish to move to Europe and the US in order to escape desperate poverty and misery make enormous personal sacrifices, and they have no outside assistance. The principle behind providing an incentive in the case of the Jewish population is simply to initiate a process that might gain its own momentum over time. In the case of South Africa, many migrated to Europe, the US, Canada and Australia, but the bulk of the population decided to stay in the country under a new dispensation. The advantage the Israeli Jews would have, in the scenario presented here (over the

DEVELOPMENT AND GLOBALISATION

white South Africans), is that they would still have the option of creating a 'state' of Israel in the new location to which they could migrate as part of an internationally agreed settlement of the present crisis.

To understand why this is not such a stretch in imagination, it is necessary to repeat a bit of history here. The British were mandated a trusteeship over Palestine by the League of Nations. It is clear that the British violated that trust. They should have allowed for a democratic dispensation in Palestine. Instead, they suppressed the genuine aspirations of the people of Palestine, and as Arthur Koestler quoted above, says, they resorted to genocide-like brutalities on the Arabs. Surreptitiously, they encouraged Jewish immigration into Palestine and trained the Jewish militia that became the core of Haganah, later the Israel Defence Forces, which defeated the Arabs in 1948. In 1947, the UN created the state of Israel, and the British coyly abstained from the vote, to send signals to the Arabs that their oil interests must be protected. The UN vote was forced on the people of Palestine undemocratically and with the force of arms at a time when the UN was dominated by US and Europe. It is now a different UN. A settlement along the lines suggested above would have the backing of a good majority of the members of the UN and provide it with the legitimacy that the 1947 partition of Palestine lacked.

There is one more important historical detail that might be worth remembering. When the League mandated the British to take over Palestine under its trusteeship, although the US backed UN Resolution 181, the US Department of State recommended the creation of the trusteeship with limits on Jewish immigration and a division of Palestine into separate Jewish and Arab provinces – not states. The two-state solution has failed. The Palestinians should have their democratic right to create their one state, as should have happened had the British been faithful to their mandate. As for the Jews, they can create, following the above referred recommendation of the US Department of State, a 'province' or in the language of the US Constitution the 'state' of 'Israel' with the difference that it should be in the United States and not in the Middle East – somewhere between Utah and California.

This is only an idea. The left in Europe and the US have proposed the boycott of Israel to force it to create a geographically contiguous state of Palestine in place of the present apartheid-like fragmented Palestine. This might have worked ten years ago. Now it is too little, too late. Its continual espousal by the left in the US and Europe blocks progress towards thinking of more imaginative and realistic alternatives.

Notes

1. National Intelligence Council (2008), *Global Trends 2025: A Transformed World*, November, www.dni.gov/nic/NIC_2025_project.html, accessed 16 January 2009.
2. http://trade.ec.europa.eu/doclib/docs/2006/october/tradoc_130376.pdf, accessed 2 July 2009.
3. See Yash Tandon (2008) *Ending Aid Dependence*, Geneva and Oxford, South Centre and Fahamu.
4. UNHRC (2009) *Special Session of Human Rights Council adopts resolution on grave human rights violations in Gaza Strip*, press release: 'In the resolution, which was adopted by a vote of 33 to 1 with 13 abstentions, the Council called for the immediate cessation of Israeli military attacks throughout the Palestinian Occupied Territory; demanded the occupying power, Israel, to immediately withdraw its military forces from the occupied Gaza Strip; called upon the occupying power to end its occupation to all Palestinian lands occupied since 1967, and to respect its commitment within the peace process towards the establishment of the independent sovereign Palestinian state with east Jerusalem as its capital; demanded that the occupying power stop the targeting of civilians and medical facilities and staff as well as the systematic destruction of cultural heritage; demanded further that the occupying power lift the siege, open all borders; and decided to dispatch an urgent independent international fact-finding mission to investigate all violations of international human rights law and international humanitarian law by the occupying power against the Palestinian people throughout the Occupied Palestinian Territory. The Council also requested the United Nations Secretary-General to investigate the latest targeting of UNRWA facilities in Gaza, including schools, that resulted in the killing of tens of Palestinian civilians, including women and children.'
5. *Haaretz* (2007) 21 October.
6. See *Middle East Economic Digest* (2001) 5 January.
7. *The Times* (2007) 23 May.
8 See Michel Chossudovsky (2006) 'The war on Lebanon and the battle for oil', *Global Research*, 23 July; and (2009) 'War and natural gas: the Israeli invasion and Gaza's offshore gas fields', *Global Research*, 8 January.
9. See Barak Ravid (2008) 'Operation Cast Lead: Israeli Air Force strike followed months of planning', *Haaretz*, 27 December.
10. Arthur Koestler (1949) *Promise and Fulfilment: Palestine 1917–1949*, London, Macmillan.
11. See *United States Department of State/Foreign Relations of the United States*,

1948. The Near East, South Asia, and Africa, vol. 5, part 2.

12. See Richard Curtis (ed) (2003) *Washington Report on Middle East Affairs, Press for Conversion Issue,* no.51, May.

13. Aljazeera.net (2009) 'Israel accused of Gaza "genocide"', 14 January, http://english.aljazeera.net/news/americas/2009/01/200911321467988347.html, accessed 2 July 2009.

14. See Benny Morris (2009) 'Why Israel feels threatened', *Financial Times,* 1 January.

15. Steven M. Cohen and Ari Y. Kelman with Lauren Blitzer (2007) *Beyond Distancing: Young Adult American Jews and Their Alienation from Israel,* Andrea and Charles Bronfman Philanthropies, http://www.acbp.net/About/PDF/Beyond%20Distancing.pdf, accessed 2 July 2009.

16. CBS (2009) *60 Minutes Exposing Israeli Apartheid,* 29 January, http://stopwar.org.uk/index.php?option=com_content&task=view&id=1037&Itemid=199.

17. See Chris Hedges (2009) 'The language of death', 12 January, http://www.truthdig.com/report/item/20090112_the_language_of_death, accessed 2 July 2009.

18. *The Economist* (2006) 10 January.

19. *Time* (2009) 19 January, vol. 173, no. 2.

20. A study conducted by the Central Intelligence Agency (CIA) has cast doubt over Israel's survival beyond the next 20 years The CIA report predicts 'an inexorable movement away from a two-state to a one-state solution, as the most viable model based on democratic principles of full equality that sheds the looming spectre of colonial apartheid while allowing for the return of the 1947/1948 and 1967 refugees. The latter being the precondition for sustainable peace in the region' (quoted from 'CIA report: Israel will fall in 20 years', http://www.care2.com/news/member/198234727/1083685, accessed 2 July 2009).

Part III
Role of the South Centre: recalling Nyerere

8

The role of the South Centre: recalling Nyerere

1 March 2009

Mwalimu Julius Nyerere, the first president of Tanzania and the founding father of the South Centre, defined development as a continuous and long struggle for liberation from structures of domination and control, and for the right and access to decision-making agencies and processes that affect the life and livelihood of the individual, the community, the nation and the region. He practised what he preached; he was one of that rare breed of philosopher-kings. In his numerous writings (from 1963 to 1999), he elaborated on the objectives and processes of these struggles as being in essence:

- Building self-confidence
- Realising the potential for self-support and contributing to society
- Leading lives of dignity, which include gainful employment that helps individuals to meet basic needs, security, equity and participation, leading to self-fulfilment
- Freedom from fear of want and exploitation
- Freedom from political, economic and social exploitation.

By contrast, development in the current mainstream dogma of neoliberal globalisation boils down to 'growth', which itself is further reduced to economics, and then even further reduced to the doctrines of the free market. This scaling down of development is further subjected to the reality on the ground where everything from trade to home mortgages is subjected to the control of banks and financial speculators – what we elsewhere called the 'financialisation of development'. This reductionist logic of financialised capitalism is the fundamental cause of the contemporary, almost total breakdown of the global financial system and with it the global system of production and exchange.

It is time to return to the basics of development as defined by Nyerere. Development does not come from outside of the self, the community and the nation. Mwalimu Nyerere's idea of creating *ujaama* villages – community structures based on traditional values of socialism and popular democracy – came under criticism even at the time. But, in retrospect, it is necessary to recognise that Ujaama had the germ of a visionary society of the future, one that is free from capitalist exploitation. One of the pioneers of this idea in practice was Ntimbanjayo Millinga, who inspired the people of his region, Ruvuma, to build *ujaama* villages. With hardly any funding from outside, the people had created 17 *ujaama* villages by 1969, which formed the Ruvuma Development Association (RDA) – an extraordinary feat of creating rural socialist communities based on self-development, and equity between women and men, and young and old. Unfortunately, internal debate within the ruling party led to the closure of the RDA, and Millinga died a disappointed man in 2008. As I write these words, women and men are gathering in Dar es Salaam to remember Millinga and Nyerere's legacy, and to revive the idea that development is primarily an outcome of the struggle by the people themselves.

What is valid at the village and national levels is valid also at the larger international and global level. In the 1980s, Nyerere chaired the South Commission set up by the developing countries, the so-called G77 countries. In its final report, *The Challenge to the South* (Oxford University Press, 1990), the commission concluded:

> For its own sake and for the sake of humanity, the South has to be resolute in resisting the present moves by the dominant countries of the North to design the system to their own advantage (p. 285).

And that, alas, has been the history of the last 30 years of neoliberal globalisation; it is a system designed to serve primarily the interest of the dominant countries of the North. Now that the system is finally crumbling, it is time to recall the essential message of the South Commission. On 31 March 1993, Nyerere paid a visit to New Delhi where he summarised that message in these five headings:

- Development shall be people centred
- Pursue a policy of maximum national self-reliance
- Supplement that with a policy of maximum collective South–South self-reliance
- Build maximum South–South solidarity in your relations with the North
- Develop science and technology.

A plaque inscribing the above five points, in Nyerere's hand writing, decorates one of the walls at the South Centre in Geneva.

The essays in this book *Daring to Think Differently*, although written as editorials over a period of 18 months, have been inspired by the legacy and teachings of Nyerere and that entire generation of third world leaders that emerged out of the struggle for emancipation from colonial and imperial rule. Of course, there were differences in strategy and tactics between them, and the struggles in their respective countries were conditioned by the historical circumstances and political and structural limitations. But they were able to unite in a movement – the Non-Aligned Movement (NAM) – which was a major force that kept them, as far as it was practically and politically possible, out of the entanglements of the cold war.

At the 14th Summit Conference of Heads of State or Government of the Non-Aligned Movement in Cuba in 2006, the South Centre was granted observer status. As Executive Director of the South Centre, I addressed the meeting in which I recalled the vision of the founding fathers of NAM, and related the role of the South Centre in the following terms:

> The primary objective of the South Centre is to promote South–South solidarity, and North–South dialogue and understanding. Like the Non-Aligned Movement, the South Centre thus promotes a community of culture and tolerance. There is still not enough recognition on the part of those who hold

power and the purse strings of the UN and the Bretton Woods Institutions that the world has changed. These institutions must reconfigure themselves to recognise the new realities on the ground. Above all, there is need to build an atmosphere of trust and confidence among the countries of the world, both in the North as well as in the south. They must recognise that every country has a right to develop its own institutions, and every nation a right to secure its own destiny. Mutual trust and tolerance for the coexistence of different systems in the world is the key to a more peaceful and just world. These must be based in the context of the accountability of governments to their people and to the recognition of the universality of human rights, including the right to development.

The Non-Aligned Movement is alive, despite doomsayers. Its essential message remains poignant and relevant even today. The challenge, as we face this new shattered world that was built on the false gods of commoditisation and financialisation of everything from human labour to climate change, is to re-design the structures of global governance such that people, not banks, control their destiny. Leaders are there to facilitate, not block as so often happens, the efforts of the people. Nyerere was such a leader. Beneath his small physical stature and simplicity lay a powerful intellect and a visionary sprit that charmed the world from the smallest village to the largest global auditorium. He passed away on 14 October 1999, tirelessly working for peace in Africa, and nurturing what was still the fragile plant of the South Centre. The plant has grown a little taller, but it is still fragile. Member states of the centre owe it to themselves, and to the memory and legacy of Julius Nyerere, to take care of this plant. Mighty oaks were once only a seed.

The South Centre is an intergovernmental organisation of developing countries established in 1995 with its headquarters in Geneva. It has grown out of the work and experience of the South Commission and its follow-up mechanism, and from recognition of the need to enhance South–South cooperation.

In pursuing its objectives of promoting South solidarity and South–South cooperation, the South Centre provides the intellectual and policy support required by developing countries on wide-ranging issues, including trade for development, innovation and access to knowledge, climate change and global governance for development.

The centre has three principal organs to achieve the objectives of the South Centre: the council of representatives made up of the representatives of the members states; the board made up of a chairperson and nine members, all highly distinguished individuals from the South, acting in their personal capacity; and the secretariat, headed by the executive director.

Benjamin W. Mkapa, the immediate former president of Tanzania is the chairperson of the South Centre. The board members in March 2009 include Chief Emeka Anyaoku (Nigeria), Norman Girvan (Jamaica), Zhaoxing Li (China), Deepak Nayyar (India), José Antonio Ocampo (Colombia), Leticia Ramos Shahani (Philippines) and Yousef Al Zalzalah (Kuwait). Bagher Asadi (Iran) sits on the board as special guest, and the convenor of the council of representatives, Peter Black (ambassador of Jamaica in Geneva), and the vice-convenor, Abdul Samad Minty (South Africa), are ex-officio members of the board.

For detailed information about the South Centre, its activities and publications, visit the website www.southcentre.org (in English, French and Spanish).

About the author

Yash Tandon is from Uganda. He is the former executive director of the South Centre, Geneva, an intergovernmental think tank of the developing countries. He studied economics and international relations at the London School of Economics, and subsequently taught at Makerere University, Uganda, and the University of Dar es Salaam. He was also a visiting professor at various other universities. Professor Tandon's long career in national and international development spans time as a policymaker, a political activist and a public intellectual. He has written over 100 scholarly articles and has authored and edited books on wide-ranging subjects from African politics to peace and security, trade and the WTO, international economics, South–South cooperation and human rights. He currently holds the Claude Ake Chair, a joint appointment with the University of Uppsala and the Nordic Africa Institute in Sweden.

Index

Breinigsville, PA USA
02 July 2010
241094BV00005B/1/P